OSPREY AIRCRAFT OF THE ACES • 95

Polikarpov I-15, I-16 and I-153 Aces

SERIES EDITOR: TONY HOLMES

OSPREY AIRCRAFT OF THE ACES • 95

Polikarpov I-15, I-16 and I-153 Aces

Mikhail Maslov

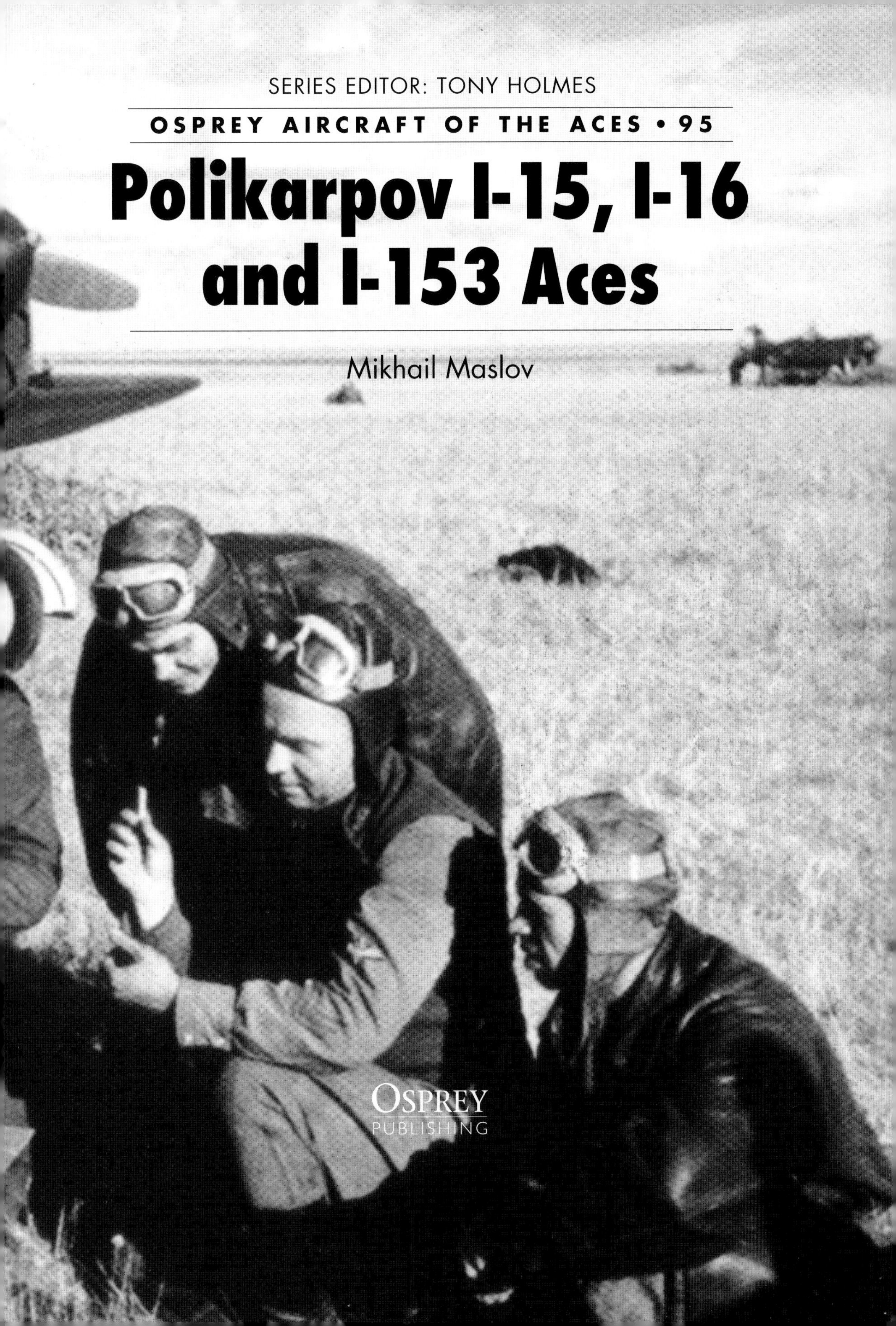

OSPREY
PUBLISHING

Front cover

The I-16 took a beating from the Jagdwaffe during the first few months of the 'Great Patriotic War', as the obsolescent fighter struggled to match the performance of the Bf 109E/F. Occasionally, however, the nimble Polikarpov fighter hit back, especially when flown by a skilled pilot such as Lt Vasiliy Golubev. On the morning of 12 March 1942 he had led his 3rd Squadron of 4th GIAP in an attack on the railway station at Mga, near Lake Lodoga. The mission was being flown in support of an offensive launched that day by the Soviet 54th Army from the southern shore of the frozen lake, which was situated near the Finnish border.

Having attacked their target without interference from German fighters, the I-16 pilots knew that they would almost certainly be bounced on their way home. In fact, the Me 109Fs of 1./JG 54 waited until the Soviet pilots were almost back over their airfield before they made their move. Golubev, who had seen combat in I-16s since the start of the war flying with the Air Force of the Baltic Fleet, had dropped slightly behind the main body of Soviet fighters so as to protect the rear of the formation. He soon spotted two Me 109Fs heading towards them above the treetops;

'A pair of enemy fighters stayed low and closed on us – they had swallowed the bait. They thought we were easy meat, but wanted to show off by shooting us down right over our own airfield. That was what I'd been waiting for. I accelerated and climbed.'

With 13 victories already to his credit, Golubev knew exactly how to get the most out of his I-16, and he soon shot the lead Bf 109 down in a head-on pass;

'I got the leader in my gunsight when he was about 500 metres away. Now I had just a second-and-a-half left – it was death or glory. The fingers of my right hand instinctively pressed the machine gun firing button and three streaks of fire pierced the slender Messerschmitt's fuselage like some magic lightning strikes. Not waiting to see the outcome, I made a sharp turn and saw the second "Messer" attempting to flee above and ahead of me. Instinctively, I pulled the firing handle, hardly bothering to assess the necessary deflection, and launched all four underwing RS-82 rockets in his direction. Four black clouds from the explosions appeared just behind the tail of the enemy fighter, but the "Messer" continued climbing steeply. I had no chance of catching him.'

A few moments later, its elevators jammed by debris from the rockets, the second Bf 109 hit the treetops and crashed on its belly on the edge of the Soviet airfield. The German pilot extricated himself from the wreckage of his fighter but subsequently died of the wounds he had received in the crash. The latter was almost certainly 26-victory ace Unteroffizier Hans Schwartzkopf, although the identity of the first pilot remains a mystery. Golubev would eventually claim 19 victories with the I-16, and survive the war with a tally of 39 and 12 shared kills to his name (*Cover artwork by Mark Postlethwaite*)

First published in Great Britain in 2010 by Osprey Publishing
Midland House, West Way, Botley, Oxford, OX2 0PH
44-02 23rd St, Suite 219, Long Island City, NY 11101, USA

E-mail; info@ospreypublishing.com

ISBN 13; 978 1 84603 981 2

Edited by Bruce Hales-Dutton and Tony Holmes
Page design by Tony Truscott
Cover Artwork by Mark Postlethwaite
Aircraft Profiles and Scale Drawings by Andrey Yurgenson
Index by Alan Thatcher
Originated by PDQ Digital Media Solutions
Printed and bound in China through Bookbuilders

10 11 12 13 14   10 9 8 7 6 5 4 3 2 1

FOR A CATALOGUE OF ALL BOOKS PUBLISHED BY OSPREY MILITARY AND AVIATION PLEASE CONTACT:

Osprey Direct, c/o Random House Distribution Center,
400 Hahn Road, Westminster, MD 21157
Email: uscustomerservice@ospreypublishing.com

Osprey Direct, The Book Service Ltd, Distribution Centre,
Colchester Road, Frating Green, Colchester, Essex, CO7 7DW
E-mail: customerservice@ospreypublishing.com

www.ospreypublishing.com

CONTENTS

INTRODUCTION

This book tells the story of the Soviet aces who flew the I-15, I-16 and I-153 series of fighters, designed by Nikolay Polikarpov. Production of the different versions of his iconic aircraft exceeded 16,000 examples, and although they were actively deployed by the VVS RKKA (*Voenno-Vozdushnye Sily Raboche Krestiyanskoy Krasnoy Armii* – Air Force of the Workers' and Peasants' Red Army) for more than a decade, their most active years in frontline service spanned 1936 to 1942.

During this period hundreds and even thousands of the fighters participated in regional conflicts and in the fighting that followed the German invasion in June 1941 to begin what the Soviets called the Great Patriotic War.

But before starting the story of the aces who flew and fought in these aircraft, it is necessary to consider some critical background issues. The most important of these centres on the actual number of combat victories attributable to individual pilots, especially those who accumulated five or more kills, thus entitling them to be classified as aces. In the years under review the VVS RKKA, like the rest of Soviet society, was permeated by the desire to subordinate the individual to the collective. The achievements of individual pilots were therefore often ignored, and it was only the scores of entire units that were publicly promoted.

Aircraft were not allocated to particular pilots, which in turn meant that they carried no individual markings or personal insignia. Reported cases of easily recognisable machines were therefore the exception rather than the rule. In the frontline pilots often switched between aircraft within the same unit for practical rather than organisational or cultural reasons. Large numbers of aircraft left the factories in sub-standard quality, and frequent failures required on-site repair. This meant regular changes of aircraft for the pilots concerned.

Yet no political system or cultural considerations could conceal a truly outstanding talent, so the most skilful – and lucky – pilots clearly stood out from the rest. Paradoxically, there was a tendency to exaggerate the success of such aviators, and to attribute heroic acts and achievements to them for propaganda purposes. This has complicated the process of extracting and verifying actual data and events and, moreover, has also cast doubts on previously published material.

Another factor that needs to be taken into account is the vast geographical span of events, their intensive nature and the mass of personalities and facts involved. Obviously, the most important facts to be extracted from this mountain of information should be those with the most historical significance. The narrative should therefore begin with a description of the aircraft flown by the aces, together with their key characteristics and production numbers.

The I-15 sesquiplane and I-16 monoplane were developed in the early 1930s by their originator, the aircraft designer Nikolay Polikarpov – a man then at the peak of his creative potential. The author has studied Polikarpov's designs for decades, leading him to believe that there are

Nikolay Polikarpov, the designer of the I-15 and I-16 series of fighters, learns to fly in a Po-2 two-seater trainer at the airfield of Factory No 39. Standing behind him is M Tarakanovsky, lead engineer of the NII (Scientific Research Institute) VVS RKKA, while instructor V Bolotnikov occupies the rear seat

The second I-15 prototype (TsKB-3), with enlarged vertical tail and modified Townend ring engine cowling, was photographed at Kacha Flying School airfield, in the Crimea, during State testing in April 1934

certain important facts about his creations that should be pointed out. In particular, statements concerning the similarity of the I-15 to the American Curtiss Hawk family of biplane fighters, which have circulated for years, are unfounded. This observation has nothing to do with any desire by the author to support his compatriot.

The fact is that the I-15 was a logical development of Polikarpov's earlier 2I-N1, I-3, I-5 and I-6 fighters. During the decade before the emergence of the I-15 and I-16, he had been consistently improving and building upon his basic concept and refining it to suit Soviet aircraft-manufacturing techniques. During this time the optimal proportions were sought between wing area and control surface area and between physical dimensions and weights, taking into account the different types of engine used to power the fighters.

The creation of aircraft of mixed metal and wood construction had more to do with the fact that rival manufacturer Andrey Tupolev had patented metal construction methods than to any preference on Polikarpov's part. He would no doubt have preferred to design all-metal aircraft of duralumin construction, but such methods had already been patented by Tupolev.

Some historians have suggested there is a link between the American Gee Bee aerobatic aircraft and the I-16, but this does not stand up to close analysis. Granted, both types were stubby, radial-engined monoplanes that were quite demanding to fly. However, the Gee Bee, which was designed for racing and beating speed records, had a dangerously small wing area that resulted in it suffering a number of accidents during its relatively short active life. The I-16's wing area was strictly in line with Polikarpov's target weight of 100 kg per square metre, although the position of the aircraft's centre of gravity resulted in poor in-flight stability but a high level of manoeuvrability. The latter meant that the first I-16 Type 5 could complete a barrel-roll in an unrivalled one to one-and-half seconds, although the rates of g associated with such manoeuvres were almost too much for even the strongest of pilots.

There were obvious parallels between Soviet and US fighters of the period since aircraft designers in both countries favoured radial powerplants, although it is true to say that at the time of the I-15's appearance aero-engine design in

The first I-16 prototype fitted with the M-22 engine was known as the TsKB-12, and it too is seen at the Kacha Flying School during State testing in April 1934

The second I-16 prototype (designated the TsKB-12bis), fitted with a Wright Cyclone F-2 engine and skis rather than a conventional wheeled undercarriage, commenced flight-testing in January 1934. Seated in the cockpit of the aircraft is Valeriy Chkalov, who had recently been transferred from the NII VVS RKKA to Polikarpov to join its team of factory test pilots. Although he later earned fame following his Arctic flight from the Soviet Union to North America in an ANT-25 in 1937, his true calling was flight-testing fighters. Chkalov flew many Polikarpov aircraft up until he was killed on 15 December 1938 during the first flight of the I-180 fighter

the Soviet Union lagged behind that of western countries. This situation had been inherited from tsarist Russia and aggravated by the 1917 Revolution and the subsequent Civil War, which caused the USSR's engineering and manufacturing capabilities to fall further behind those of leading European nations and the USA. The gap would take decades to overcome, and the result was that until the Soviet Union could catch up, all engines had to be imported.

As a professional aircraft designer, Polikarpov was well aware of both the difficulties faced by Soviet aero-engine manufacturers and the advances being made abroad. His first fighters were powered by imported Liberty, Napier and BMW liquid-cooled inline engines, but in the 1920s the prevailing opinion among aircraft designers was that fighters should be powered by air-cooled radials. In the USSR, therefore, the British 480 hp Bristol Jupiter was put into production as the M-22. Between 1926 and 1928 Polikarpov produced several designs incorporating the M-22, but his requests for access to the engine were denied due to the manoeuvrings of Tupolev, who was able to persuade the CAHI (Central Aero- and Hydrodynamics Institute) to grant him exclusive entitlement to the unit.

However, by the early 1930s Polikarpov was able to gain access to the M-22, allowing early I-16s to be equipped with this powerplant. But the most successful versions of his famous fighter were the later ones fitted with American engines, the first examples of which were imported in 1930. In 1932-33, after a series of negotiations, Soviet representatives acquired the necessary tooling and a licence from Curtiss-Wright to manufacture the 625 hp Cyclone R-1820-F3 engine in a new factory built in Perm, in the Ural region.

Arkady Shvetsov, chief designer in charge of adapting the Wright Cyclone for manufacture in the USSR, had personally participated in the acquisition of the first engines and the tooling. Initially, in 1934, the Perm Cyclones were assembled from American-made parts, but the following year, the plant, now designated Aircraft Factory No 19, mastered the entire process and was able to start turning out a completely Soviet product. By the end of 1935 660 engines, now designated the M-25 in compliance with the Soviet system, had been completed.

The TsKB-3 (I-15) sesquiplane and TsKB-12 (I-16) monoplane were developed for this engine, both fighter prototypes having been fully

flight-tested by the end of 1933 and put into production the following year. During state tests, the I-15 demonstrated an ability to reach a maximum speed of 230 mph and to climb to 16,250 ft in 6.2 minutes. The fighter could also complete a 360-degree turn in just eight seconds. The new aircraft was duly acknowledged as having better performance than any existing Soviet fighter. Indeed, from the standpoints of manoeuvrability and rate of climb, the I-15 was far ahead

of any of its contemporaries, while its speed at 16,250 ft almost matched the best foreign machines. All these factors led to the M-25-powered I-15 being recommended for series production at Moscow-based factories Nos 1 (where 384 were subsequently built) and 39.

The first series-produced I-15s began to reach VVS RKKA units towards the end of 1934, although they did not enter frontline service until mid-1935. The first units to deploy the new fighters included the Special Purpose Air Brigade at Lyubertsy (Moscow region) and fighter squadrons based in Kiev, Bryansk, Bobruysk and Spassk Dalniy, in the Far East region.

Although pleased to be flying such modern fighters, I-15 pilots routinely had to endure mechanical failures and breakdowns. There were frequent reports of poor assembly and quality of materials. The powerful M-25 engines were mounted in the airframe without any dampers, resulting in serious vibration overstressing the entire machine. Fuel tanks often leaked and sometimes caused in-flight fires. The propeller's starting gear tended to break off, and the propellers themselves demonstrated very short lives. Grass cut by the wheel spats tended to become wrapped around axles until it produced a sudden braking effect, which sometimes resulted in nose-overs on landing. Suffice it to say the I-15's introduction into service was accompanied by many difficulties.

In 1935 those problems even resulted in production being halted while the more serious faults were eliminated. The latter included poor longitudinal stability at speeds in excess of 155 mph caused by the gull-shaped upper wing centre section, which resulted in the fighter's unofficial name of *Chaika* (Seagull). Efforts to improve the I-15 were conducted in parallel with the delivery of the first I-16s to military units. Inevitably, commanders favoured the more modern aircraft, and the decision was taken to cease I-15 production in 1935.

Quantity production of the I-16 was started in 1934 at Aircraft Factory No 21 at Gorkiy, now Nizhniy Novgorod. Initially, the

The TsKB-12 fitted with the M-22 engine was put into production with the designation I-16 Type 4 in 1934 at Factory No 21 at Gorkiy, now Nizhniy Novgorod. This particular example does not feature the normal drop-down panel on the left side of the cockpit to facilitate entry

TsKB-12 prototype construction number 123954 was photographed near the hangar doors at Factory No 39 shortly after it was rolled out on 25 April 1935. Sometimes referred to in documents as 'aircraft No 54', its distinctive features included an improved engine cowling with adjustable cooling shutters, modified aileron mountings and flap-type fairings on the tail control surfaces. During factory testing 'aircraft No 54' had a take-off weight of 3194 lbs and reached a maximum speed of 283 mph at 9750 ft. This aircraft became the prototype for the highly successful I-16 Type 5, which was the first version of Polikarpov's monoplane fighter to be fitted with the more powerful 625 hp M-25 engine, rather than the 480 hp M-22

aircraft was powered by the M-22 engine, with the more powerful and modern M-25 unit being reserved for the I-14 fighter designed by Andrey Tupolev's design bureau at CAHI. However, by the summer of 1935 it was discovered that the M-25-powered I-16 outperformed the I-14, resulting in the latter's cancellation after just 22 examples had been built. The following year the manufacture of M-25-powered I-16s began.

The first fighter in the world to be built in such large numbers, a total of 10,292 I-16s (including the UTI-4 trainer version) were manufactured between 1934 and 1942, as shown by the table below;

Factory	1934	1935	1936	1937	1938	1939	1940	1941	1942	Subtotal
No 39 (Moscow)	50	4	4	-	-	-	-	-	-	**58**
No 21 (Gorkiy)	-	527	902	1881	1070	1571	2207	336	-	**8494**
No 153 (Novosibirsk)	-	-	-	6	105	264	503	423	-	**1301**
No 458 (Rostov-on-Don*)	-	-	-	-	-	-	-	356	83	**439**
Total:	**50**	**531**	**906**	**1887**	**1175**	**1835**	**2710**	**1115**	**83**	**10,292**

(*Factory No 458 built the UTI-4 trainer variant only)

A successful combat debut in the Spanish Civil War gave both the I-15 and I-16 a new lease of life. For the latter fighter, it resulted in the production of several new versions powered by the M-25V (Types 10 and 17), M-62 (Types 18, 24 and 27) and M-63 (Types 24, 28 and 29) engines. The I-15 was modified as the I-15bis, lacking the characteristic gull-wing shape, but it proved to be a mediocre performer. This was highlighted in a series of mock battles performed by pilots of the Air Force Scientific Research Institute (NII VVS) in late September 1937. A mock attack on the prototype ANT-42 heavy bomber from above and behind at 8125-9750 ft resulted in the I-15bis losing height and failing to match the four-engined bomber's speed. Accordingly, the fighter was branded as 'completely ineffective'. The Institute's report concluded;

'In the air combat environment the I-15 has no advantages over the I-16. There are even difficulties in breaking off combat. All the

The original gull wing that characterised early I-15s was singled out for criticism by many pilots who stated that it restricted their view from the cockpit. It was also found to decrease longitudinal stability at speeds above 155 mph. The VVS RKKA duly requested that these problems be corrected, and Polikarpov redesigned the I-15 by fitting a normal strutted upper wing. In this photograph, the TsKB-3 No 7 prototype is seen at Factory No 1 during flight-testing in March 1935. Production aircraft with this wing layout were designated I-15bis

An I-15bis of 13th OIAE of the Baltic Fleet Air Force has its M-25V engine started up prior to the fighter conducting a pre-war training flight. Note the wooden chocks under the wheels and the mounting tabs for the wheel spat visible on the right side of the farthest wheel. The spats were usually removed from frontline aircraft

The I-152 was regarded as the standard version of the I-15 for 1938 production, replacing the I-15bis. Although essentially the same as the latter aircraft, it had individual exhaust pipes and a three-panel windscreen, among other modest improvements. The I-152 designation was only used for a short while, and simultaneously with the development of the significantly different I-153 project. The report created following flight-testing of the I-152 during the summer of 1938 concluded that the fighter should have appeared six months earlier. This in turn meant that it did not go into production, being supplanted by the I-153. Examples of the latter fighter started to reach the VVS RKKA in the early summer of 1939

advantages in air combat are with the I-16. The I-15 is somewhat better from the standpoint of time-to-climb and manoeuvrability, while the I-15bis, only by virtue of the M-25V engine's power reserves, can break off combat by diving away.'

Despite the negative reports, development of the I-15bis continued, and the total number built reached an impressive 2408 in 1938-39. The aircraft stayed in production because Polikarpov promised prompt and adequate improvement to allow it to remain effective as a fighter. Indeed, a proposed new version featuring retractable landing gear was completed by the company in the autumn of 1937. Initially, it was referred to as the 'I-15bis standard version for 1938 production', but this designation was subsequently applied to a modified I-15bis that was eventually identified as the I-152. The variant with retractable landing gear, initially known as the 'I-15, 3rd version', was later designated the I-153.

Although the I-152 did not go into production, the I-15bis and I-153 were to become widely known. The unofficial name of *Chaika*, which had originally been used just to describe the upward-cranked upper wing centre section, later became the sesquiplane's official name.

State testing of the I-153 fitted with a 1000 hp M-62 engine began in June 1939. The fighter reached a maximum speed of 275 mph at 15,000 ft, could complete a 360-degree turn in 13 to 13.5 seconds and had a service ceiling of 31,850 ft. However, a maximum speed of at least 285 mph had been expected, and the I-153 M-62 failed to pass the State acceptance tests. The VVS RKKA also demanded better cockpit visibility, together with a number of minor modifications.

Despite these problems, the aircraft was put into production in the autumn of 1939 at one of the USSR's best aircraft-building facilities, Factory No 1, located just 15 minutes from the Kremlin. By the end of the year, 1011 I-153s had been completed and handed over to the VVS RKKA. A further 189 *Chaikas* with M-63 engines were not completed, these being rescheduled for construction in 1940 when the target of 2040 I-153s was exceeded by 322 aircraft. The final 64 were built in 1941 to complete production of Soviet biplane fighters. The total output of I-153s between 1939 and 1941 amounted to 3437 fighters.

In 1940 the VVS RKKA units of the Red Army and Navy received 2005 I-153 fighters. As at 20-25 September 1940, the total number in

This first series I-153 fighter, fitted with an M-63 engine, was photographed sitting on its ski undercarriage between test flights in early 1939

Red Army Air Force service, including fighters supplied in 1939, included 2135 M-62- and 304 M-63-powered I-153s. By then the Naval Air Force had received 217 M-62-powered I-153s and nine fitted with the M-63. Meanwhile, Polikarpov's other creation, the I-16, was being delivered to military units in similarly large numbers, as detailed below;

Type	1938	1939	1940
I-15bis	1104	1304	-
I-153	-	1011	2362
I-16*	716	1147	1607

(*Only I-16s intended for combat are included, UTI-4 trainers being excluded)

According to a report issued by the Red Army Air Force Department on 14 September 1939, combat units had 4478 fighters (5082 when the aircraft flown by training units were included) at their disposal as follows – 2256 I-16s with machine guns, 245 I-16s with cannon, 160 I-153s, 1642 I-15bis, five I-16s able to carry rocket projectiles, 12 I-14s and 158 DI-6s.

As of 20-25 September 1940 the Red Army Air Force had a grand total of 8636 fighters at its disposal as follows – 2872 M-25 I-16s, 248 M-62 I-16s, 1234 M-63 I-16s, 1807 M-25 I-15s, 2135 M-62 I-153s and 304

A mixed group of I-16 Type 5 and Type 24 fighters prepare to have their engines turned over using Hucks starters – a scene reminiscent of aviation in World War 1

These rather elderly I-16 Type 5s, with sliding cockpit canopies and camera guns, were operated by 61st IAB of the Baltic Fleet Air Force in the late 1930s. The fighters' engine cowlings were painted in black, which was a departure from the colour scheme specified for aircraft built at Factory No 39. The Department of the Air Force protested against this unauthorised deviation from the standard green/light blue scheme, although some air force units continued to operate aircraft with black-painted engine cowlings

Five all-red I-16 Type 24s of an unidentified VVS RKKA aerobatic team form up on the wing of an accompanying UTI-4 (a two-seat version of the I-16 Type 5). During the late 1930s every military district of the Soviet Union was able to boast an I-16 aerobatic team. Participation in such 'parade fives' was considered to be a great honour, and many pilots did their best to be selected

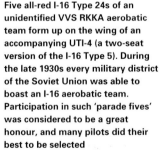

M-63 I-153s. Additionally, as of September 1940, training units and flight schools had the following aircraft on their strength – 227 M-22 I-16s, 22 M-22 UTI-2s and 1047 M-25 UTI-4s.

The inventory of 'miscellaneous aircraft' included 14 I-14 and 22 IP-1 single-seat monoplane fighters and 179 DI-6 two-seat biplane fighters. It should be noted that although formally included in unit inventories, both the I-14 and IP-1 had already been taken out of service, and surviving examples would soon be discarded. The DI-6 two-seaters were also of little practical value, and they would never participate in significant combat operations.

According to the Red Army Air Force Department report to the Defence Committee of the USSR Council of People's Commissars on 14 May 1940, air force combat units at 1 January 1940 included 63 fighter regiments. A Defence Council decree called for the creation of 35 more air regiments, and by the end of May 22 of these had been formed.

In the Naval Air Force the following fighters and trainers were available on 1 October 1940 – 341 M-25 I-16s, 36 M-62 I-16s, 174 M-63 I-16s, 335 M-25 I-15s, 217 M-62 I-153s, 9 M-63 I-153s, 129 M-25 UTI-4s and 3 M-22 UI-2s.

These figures imply that during the three years before the outbreak of war, Red Army Air Force units received about 10,000 new fighters, including almost 4000 in 1940 alone. Although they were obsolescent in

terms of flight and combat performance when compared to western fighter types such as the Hurricane, Spitfire and Bf 109E, the Polikarpovs supported the concept of 'mass', which held that the enemy would be overwhelmed by sheer weight of numbers rather than by the quality of the weapons deployed. In practice huge quantities of fighters were turned out, but at the expense of quality.

Pilots from an unidentified Baltic Fleet Air Force unit relax near one of their I-16s in the summer of 1940. Such scenes were a rarity once war erupted in the east on 22 June 1941

Until 1940 most units were staffed by well-trained and experienced pilots, many of whom had combat experience in Spain, China or Mongolia. But this was diluted by the hurried formation of new units in 1940-41, which resulted in experienced fighter pilots being given commands for which they were unsuited. Completing the training of the fresh pilots now graduating from flying schools without sufficient time in the cockpit and lacking essential flying skills proved to be a further headache for unit COs.

And the growing armada of aircraft was short of airfields, since many of those planned were still in the process of construction, renovation or expansion. There was also a shortage of fuel, which cut flying hours. In spite of efforts to save fuel, by the summer of 1941 many units had only enough for a few days of combat operations. Another consideration was engine hours, which could soon be used up by training flights, leaving little life for combat operations.

Below and bottom
'Scramble!' Pilots rush to their I-153s at an airfield near Leningrad in the winter of 1941-42 . . . and their commander prepares to give them the signal to take-off by firing a flare into the air

On top of all this, an unusually harsh winter in 1940-41 further hindered pilot training at operational units, even though thousands of flying school graduates continued to arrive – the air force of the Leningrad Military District alone received 700 new pilots in the autumn of 1940. But some trainees arrived at units that possessed nothing but an identification number and command personnel.

In the spring of 1941 the most experienced pilots began converting to the new LaGG-3, MiG-3 and Yak-1 fighters, leaving them with little spare time to help younger squadronmates master operational flying in the less than forgiving I-16 and I-153.

This I-15bis is seen in its well-weathered white winter camouflage scheme on a snow-covered airfield on the Leningrad Front in late 1941. As can clearly be seen here, in cold conditions the M-25V engine had to be warmed up with the help of a heater and thermal covers before it could be started

All of these issues, combined with inadequate communications, logistical support and airfield management, had a negative impact on the combat performance of the VVS RKKA in June 1941. Yet Soviet pilots still managed to ensure that the Jagdwaffe did not have things entirely its own way during the first weeks of the war in the east. A handbook called *Fighter Aircraft Tactics*, prepared in 1942 and published early the following year, contained this advice for fighter pilots;

'The I-16 is, of course, slower than the Me 109, but it is more manoeuvrable. The I-16 pilot cannot therefore force a "Messer" into combat if the latter's pilot is unwilling to fight, but an enemy willing to fight can easily be beaten by the I-16. In turn, the I-16 can also avoid combat with an attacking Me 109 if its pilot spots the enemy in good time. Usually, the I-16 should engage the Me 109 in a head-on attack. For the I-16, as with any other fighter type, a significant advantage can be gained by being above enemy aircraft. When attacking the Me 109 from ahead and above, the latter's pilot is helpless. Being above the enemy, the I-16 may make a diving attack from behind. This means that I-16 units must ensure that at least one element is always above the enemy fighters.'

Loss rates for the new MiG, Yak and LaGG fighters during the first year of the war were comparable to those of the I-16 and I-153. That resulted in proposals for the resumption of I-16 and I-153 production, which was still under serious consideration as late as the second half of 1942. Air Marshal Aleksander Novikov, Commander of the Red Army Air Force during this period, received an urgent summons to General Headquarters on 26 September 1942 to discuss the proposal. He recalled;

'S Khudyakov (Commander of the Western Front Air Force), supported by N Bulganin of the Military Council, wrote a letter to Joseph Stalin in September 1942 calling for the production of the I-16 and I-153. Khudyakov's letter was originated by Nemtsovich, Commander of the Fighter Air Division. Having read it, Stalin summoned Khudyakov and Bulganin to hear their opinion on the matter, but he disagreed with them. So he decided to recall me from the frontline for further discussions before making a decision.

'I met Stalin on 28 September. He told me that Khudyakov and Bulganin were eager to resume I-16 and I-153 production, but that he disagreed. I told him that the I-16 and I-153 performed well in defensive situations, but that they were not suitable for offensive operations. And since we were planning a major offensive, we needed to achieve dominance of the air. This meant that further production of the I-16 and I-153 should be abandoned. Stalin agreed with my arguments, and the old fighters would never be built again.'

This episode represented the last time that production of the I-16 and I-153 was seriously contemplated. From then on only spare parts and repair kits were shipped to the frontline to facilitate the survival of the remaining aircraft.

SPANISH CIVIL WAR

During the civil war in Spain the I-15 and I-16 became the first Soviet-built fighters to encounter their foreign counterparts in actual combat conditions. Indeed, their appearance near Madrid in the autumn of 1936 dramatically changed the operational situation on the ground. Before their arrival the fighter force fielded by the socialist government (Republican) air force could only be described as poor. Indeed, most of the 48 obsolete French Nieuport-Delage Ni D 52 sesquiplane fighters on strength when the conflict started in July 1936 had been lost by November, while many of the survivors required repair. Other French fighter types such as the Dewoitine D 371/372 parasol and Loire 46 gull wing were available in insufficient quantities – 24 and five, respectively – to be regarded as a viable combat force.

In August 1936, the right-wing Nationalist force led by General Francisco Franco started to receive modern aircraft and volunteers from Nazi Germany and Fascist Italy. Junkers Ju 52/3m bomber-transports airlifted Nationalist Spanish troops in from Morocco and Heinkel He 51 and Fiat CR.32 biplane fighters seized aerial supremacy over much of Spain. The Republicans urgently called for foreign assistance to help stem Nationalist advances in the south, and the French duly supplied 60 assorted obsolescent combat aircraft. Still more German and Italian types had also arrived in Spain by year-end to counter the Republican aircraft, but it was only when the USSR agreed to supply I-15s and I-16s, as well as Tupolev SB-2 bombers, that things began to look up for the socialists. Pilots were also sent to fly them, but the Kremlin demanded full payment in gold in return for both men and materiel.

The first batch of aircraft to arrive in Spain from the Soviet Union included 40 I-15 fighters. On 28 October 1936 the steamship *Carl Lepin* docked in the Spanish Mediterranean port of Cartagena, having sailed from Sebastopol with 15 pilots, led by future ace Pavel Rychagov, and 25 dismantled I-15s. A few days later a further group of ten pilots, headed by Boris Turzhanskiy, and 15 I-15s arrived at Bilbao, in the north of Spain.

The first group was quickly sent to Alcantarilla airfield near Murcia, where the fighters were promptly assembled in an olive grove by Soviet technicians and then flight-tested. According to future ace Grigoriy Zakharov, the I-15s were assembled on the day of their arrival, 28 October. Spanish Republican markings of red wingtips and fuselage stripe and red, yellow and violet striped rudders were also hastily applied.

On 3 November 11 assembled and flight-tested I-15s were ferried to Madrid. The last to leave were those flown by Zverev and Kondratyev, and they lost their bearings in the evening twilight and, having crossed the Sierra Guadarrama, landed at an enemy airfield near Segovia. Both pilots were taken prisoner, but they were later exchanged for two captured Nationalist pilots. The remaining nine fighters reached their initial destination – the airfield at Alcalá de Henares, near Madrid, which was the main Republican air base at the time. With the arrival of the I-16s later that same month, the I-15 group was re-located to Soto.

Snr Lt Pavel Rychagov fought in Spain as commander of I-15-equipped *Escuadrilla Palancar* (his *nom de guerre* during the conflict was 'Pablo Palancar') from 20 October 1936 to 6 February 1937, during which time he personally claimed six aircraft destroyed, and shared in the destruction of 14 others. He also saw action over Lake Khasan in the summer of 1938, when Japanese and Soviet troops clashed for the first time

Evgeniy Erlykin served in Spain between October 1936 and 27 March 1937, and as an I-15 flight commander he personally accounted for several enemy aircraft destroyed during this time. He subsequently saw further combat in the Winter War as CO of 59th IAB, although he did not 'make ace'

The Spanish Republicans nicknamed the Russian sesquiplane *Chato* ('snub-nosed'), while the Nationalists, along with the rest of the international aviation community, erroneously labelled the Polikarpov-designed fighter as a 'Curtiss'. The *Chato* name stuck, and it was more frequently used than the official Spanish registration markings painted on the fuselage sides behind the cockpit. These markings, incidentally, included the code CC- or CA-, followed by a number. The CC- code was applied to Soviet-built fighters, while CA- was reserved for aircraft manufactured in Spain. The two letters were followed by a number so that, for example, CC-250 would mean that the aircraft concerned was the 250th fighter received into the inventory of the Republican air force. There were some variations, however. For instance, in 1937, in the Spanish squadron led by Andrés García Lacalle, the aircraft only displayed tactical numbers, the letters having been deleted.

Pavel Rychagov was shot down while dogfighting with CR.32s over Madrid on 16 November 1936, and while he was recovering in hospital Petr Pumpur was appointed temporary commander of the I-15 group. The two detachments were in turn led by Evgeniy Erlykin and Georgiy Zakharov. In January 1937 Aleksander Osadchiy was promoted to command the group.

It should be noted that during the initial phase of combat operations, Soviet pilots did not use the term 'squadron'. The Republicans were habitually called 'friends', and in official documents all their forces were designated as 'the blues'. The enemy was defined simply as 'the enemy', 'the fascists' or, occasionally, 'the whites'. Conversely, the Republicans were usually called 'the reds' by the Nationalists.

Before his arrival in Spain, Pavel Rychagov had served for five years as a regular fighter pilot, prior to being appointed commander of 109th IAE (*Istrebitelniy Aviatsionnaya Eskadrilya* – Fighter Aviation Squadron) of 36th IAB (*Istrebitelniy Aviatsionnaya Brigada* – Fighter Aviation Brigade) in the Kiev Military District. This suggests that he was considered to be both an experienced pilot and a promising commander. In January 1936 Snr Lt Rychagov was awarded the Order of Lenin 'for exemplary service'. He arrived in Spain on 20 October 1936 and left on 6 February 1937 with 105 flying hours recorded in his logbook during the 'foreign trip'.

Leading the I-15 fighter group throughout his brief tour of duty in Spain, Rychagov had achieved six aerial victories by 9 December 1936, making him the leading Soviet ace at that time. Before returning to the USSR (whereupon he was replaced by Ivan Kopets) he reported shooting down two more enemy fighters. On 31 December 1936 Rychagov received the title Hero of the Soviet Union and he was immediately elevated to the rank of major, bypassing that of captain.

From December 1937 to April 1938 Rychagov served as a senior military adviser in charge of Soviet air activities in China, and he later commanded the VVS RKKA detachments at Lake Khasan,

Hidden under trees, this I-15 *Chato* is about to have its engine fired up via a Hucks starter in late 1936. This aircraft was part of the first batch of 40 I-15s delivered to Spain

in Mongolia, and during the Soviet-Finnish Winter War. In the summer of 1940 Rychagov was promoted to the rank of lieutenant general of aviation and appointed Head of Red Army Air Force Administration. In December 1940 he became a member of the Red Army Chief Military Council and in February 1941 Deputy People's Commissar for Defence in charge of aviation.

However, in the spring of 1941 Rychagov was dismissed from his post, officially because of the high accident rates amongst his units, although the actual reason was that he had told Stalin 'You force us to fly wooden coffins!' at a high-level meeting. The 29-year-old ace would pay a heavy price for such insubordination. On 24 June 1941 Rychagov was arrested on a charge of being responsible for the catastrophic loss rates suffered by VVS RKKA units at the hands of the Luftwaffe in the wake of the German invasion. He and 20 other high-ranking Red Army commanders who had also fallen out with Stalin were executed on 28 October.

The first report of the I-15's operational deployment in Spain was dated 4 November 1936. On that day three air combats resulted in two Ju 52/3ms being shot down out of 12 attempting to bomb Madrid, together with two CR.32 fighters. A third Ju 52/3m and a Heinkel two-seater were damaged badly enough to make forced landings. No losses were reported among the participating I-15s, although Zakharov's aircraft was badly damaged.

During the next two days further air combats resulted in 12 more victories being reported by the Soviet pilots, but at the cost of two I-15s lost. Mitrofanov was shot down over enemy territory, and although he bailed out of his burning aircraft he was killed. Miroshnichenko had to crash-land back at base after his fighter had a gear leg shot off during the mission. The I-15 was written-off in the landing but the pilot walked away unhurt.

After less than a month of combat near Madrid the Republican fighter pilots had reported shooting down more than 60 enemy aircraft – a figure which was clearly exaggerated. Meanwhile, the number of combat-ready *Chatos* in the central area had also fallen so that by 20 November there were only 15 operational aircraft left. Seven fighters had been lost in air combat, one was undergoing repair and two had force-landed in enemy territory.

Georgiy Zakharov was another pilot to enjoy early success in these autumn actions. Like Pavel Rychagov, he was an experienced aviator who had seen service with 109th IAE of 83rd IAB prior to volunteering for combat in Spain from the Byelorussian Military District. During one of his first missions, Zakharov became detached from the rest of his unit (a 12-stong formation of I-15s led by Rychagov) and narrowly escaped being shot down by enemy fighters, as he recalled;

'Here I am above Madrid. I look around and there's no one there, neither friend or foe. Then I scrutinise the horizon in the direction of the glaring sun. With flickering eyes I finally detect the remote shapes of friendly biplanes. Stressing my vision, I manage to count them – 12! So Pavel must have decided to ensure the most favourable conditions for our attack, thus heading north of Madrid so as to lead the flight into the attack from down-sun. That's where I should have looked for them right from the start.

'They approach the city in a wide arc and I am inside that arc, so I can quickly catch up, flying headlong towards them. I want to make my way towards the leading aircraft and take up my position on Rychagov's left. Well, I've been too hasty and popped up in front of the leader. Now I need to be spotted by my comrades, so I reduce speed and rock my wings. I believe they will see me and soon catch up. What happens next I still regard as being beyond my comprehension. I will forever remember that feeling, which is hard to explain in mere words, when the burst of enemy gunfire narrowly missed cutting off my wing. However, it was instinct that saved me, rather than training or rational thinking. Before I realised where I was and what was happening I had already swerved away into a steep turn to spoil the enemy's aim. Yet I still felt I was a target, and I felt it with my entire physical being.

'Today I see that the only reason I survived was that there were too many hunters after me. The entire swarm was engaged in pursuing me and they got in each other's way. Otherwise, the first one to approach me from behind would easily have split my aircraft in two with his first burst. Instead, they all began to shoot erratically. My fighter was hit but I was alive! I was spinning between them while trying to draw them towards Madrid where, I felt, I could save myself. My comrades-in-arms would soon come to my rescue, I thought. The g-forces were almost blinding but I knew I couldn't give up and fly straight and level for more than a second! The aircraft had to withstand the punishment. I prayed that it wouldn't fall apart.

'Three times Heinkels popped up into my gunsight and I pushed the firing buttons. And here I was, finally, approaching my airfield. Well, I could do better than reveal its location to the enemy, but I had no choice. My aeroplane's bracing wires had been shot away and the wing curved upwards to the verge of collapse. I looked back, just in time to meet another blast of gunfire. My instrument panel was smashed and my upper machine guns were out of order. A Heinkel kept close behind me to finish me off, but I made it and landed from a hedgehopping approach.

'The mechanics promptly pulled me out of the cockpit and we escaped to shelter under the nearest trees. I pressed my back against a tree-trunk and suddenly felt that my lips were being wetted – oh, it was just some water from a friend's flask.'

Having survived this close shave Zakharov would subsequently claim the first of his victories on 9 November when he downed an 'Arado' bomber (actually an Italian Romeo Ro.37 reconnaissance biplane) heading for Madrid;

'On my fourth mission in Spain I brought down my first prey. That's not to say it was a great victory, just an obsolete two-seat Arado bomber also on its way to Madrid. We met above the clouds. Having noticed me, the Arado pilot swerved down to hide in a cloud but

Unidentified Soviet volunteer pilots discuss their next mission in front of an I-15 for the benefit of the camera

I was too quick. Avoiding the enemy's fire, I followed him and also dived into the clouds. Having emerged at an altitude of about 500 m (1600 ft), I started circling around and waiting for the Arado to appear. Indeed, seconds later, the bomber fell from the cloud bit by bit – a wing came first, then the fin. Whether it had been overstressed or whether it was the result of my fire, the unfortunate Arado was in pieces before it reached the ground.'

Ivan Kopets arrived in Spain in September 1936 and remained there until 17 June 1937. He took over command of the I-15 group from Pavel Rychagov when the latter returned to the USSR in February 1937. Kopets shot down several enemy aircraft, although he failed to attain ace status

Georgiy Zakharov remained in Spain until 7 April 1937, by which time he had shot down six enemy aircraft and shared in the destruction of four more. He had claimed kills both in the I-15 and I-16.

By early December 1936 the Nationalist offensive towards Madrid had slowed and small Republican fighter groups were being re-deployed to other theatres of operation. Among the first was that led by Ivan Kopets, which was moved east to the Aragon front in an effort to neutralise a group of He 51s flown by a mixed contingent of German and Spanish Nationalist pilots operating in the Teruel area. Assisted by six I-16s led by Morozov, the three *Chato* pilots performed their task to perfection. Indeed, by the end of the year they had been credited with destroying five of the six He 51s operating in the area. One had been shot down in combat and the remaining four had been destroyed on their airfield by the I-15s. However, the Nationalists also lodged equally optimistic claims against the Republican fighters in this area.

An unidentified Soviet pilot (left) and his Spanish comrade stand alongside an I-15 *Chato* that has been connected to a Hucks starter

In January 1937 two *Chato* flights commanded by Evgeniy Erlykin and Adam Kovalevskiy flew south to Malaga. A third Soviet pilot, Emelyan Kondrat, was also a member of one of the flights, but the remaining pilots were Spanish. On 1 February Kovalevskiy shot down a Savoia-Marchetti SM.81 bomber, but he was in turn fatally wounded by return fire from the burning aircraft.

In mid-February Erlykin and Kondrat were recalled to the central theatre near Madrid, and Spanish pilot Emilio Galera was promoted to detachment commander.

In December 1936 and January 1937 two more shipments of 30 I-15s arrived in Spain from the Soviet Union, making it possible to form a complete combat unit of four I-15 squadrons. It should be noted that a squadron represented the largest tactical unit within the VVS RKKA, and normally comprised 31 aircraft. In Spain, the largest unit was a group, which comprised four squadrons of ten to twelve aircraft. However, due to permanent shortages of aircraft a squadron might well comprise fewer machines, and operate independently from its parent group to meet the requirements of different field commanders.

Soviet archives offer the following picture of I-15 availability, distribution and command staff as at 15 February 1937. All four squadrons were commanded by Ivan Kopets;

Unit Commander	Ready/Under Repair	Airfield	Flight crew
Squadron Zotsenko	16/-	Alcazár de San Juan	16 Soviet pilots
Squadron Osadchiy	18/5	Almeria	12 Soviet and 6 'friendly' pilots
Squadron Lacalle	13/4	Guadalajara	8 Spanish and 4 American pilots
Squadron Alonzo	11/6	San Javier	11 Spanish pilots

Until the spring of 1937 central Spain was the main theatre of combat operations for the Polikarpov fighters – a fact reflected in the airfields listed above. On 16 February, for example, several Ju 52/3ms, He 51s and CR.32s were shot down. The I-15 units also suffered losses. That same day, American pilot, and future Polikarpov ace, Frank Tinker of Lacalle's squadron was shot down, while on the 18th three more of Lacalle's fighters and two from Zotsenko's squadron were lost. Despite these casualties, Republican aerial supremacy remained intact in central Spain.

In May 1937 another batch of 31 *Chatos* arrived from the Soviet Union, taking the total number supplied to the Republicans to 116. These new fighters greatly enhanced the strength of the I-15 group, their arrival coinciding with the return of Spanish Republican pilots who had been undergoing fighter training at the Soviet flight school near Kirovabad. They were accompanied by Soviet pilots under the command of future ace Capt Ivan Eremenko.

Initially, these new aircraft were used to fly patrols over the Mediterranean coastal zone from Cartagena and Elche to Alicante, protecting Republican warships and cargo vessels. This mission had initially been performed by the I-16, but following the redeployment of the latter type to the north, and the poor quality of the latest batch of Polikarpov fighters to reach Spain, the I-15 group was given the task of coastal patrolling. The pilots assigned this role formed the backbone of 1a Squadron, which had been placed under Capt Eremenko's command while Lacalle was undergoing further training in the Soviet Union.

Ivan Eremenko served in Spain from May 1937 to February 1938.

An I-15 has its engine warmed up at an unidentified location prior to the aircraft taking off from the ploughed-up temporary airfield

Prior to that he had been commander of 119th IAE of 95th IAB in the Transcaucasian Military District. Once in Spain Eremenko was appointed commander of the Soviet-manned I-15 squadron, and later of the entire *Chato* detachment. His combat record included 260 flight hours and nine victories, with one of the latter being a bomber that he brought down at night. Eremenko's victory tally made him the leading Soviet pilot of the campaign. On 28 October 1937, as a reward for his successes in Spain, he was awarded the title of Hero of the Soviet Union. After his return from Spain, Eremenko's career blossomed. He was immediately appointed to the post of brigade commander and was subsequently promoted further still. Eremenko would never participate in air combat again, however, undertaking administrative roles for the rest of his military career.

In July 1937 the Nationalists moved the Ju 52/3m night bomber detachment of the elite *Legion Condor* nearer to Madrid. The Republicans responded with the deployment of a nightfighter group comprising the *Chato* squadron led by Nikolay Kuznetsov, although it had been intended that Eremenko would command it. The detachment was known as the *Patrulla de Noche* (the 'Night Patrol'), and many Soviet pilots with night flying experience were assigned to it, including future ace Anatoliy Serov (soon to become group commander), Leonid Rybkin, Mikhail Yakushin and Vladimir Sorokin.

The detachment's first night victory was achieved on 27 July when, soon after midnight, the two-fighter element of Serov and Yakushin intercepted a Ju 52/3m. The latter pilot succeeded in shooting the aircraft down in flames, only one member of its crew escaping by parachute. The victory was triumphantly celebrated, with Spanish Prime Minister Juan Negrin personally congratulating the victorious pilots and presenting them each with a gold watch and a luxury car as tokens of his gratitude. Mikhail Yakushin later described his first night victory;

'At midnight we received a telephone report of an enemy bombing raid on Republican troops near El Escorial. It was the first time that we had approached the front after dark. The search area was outlined by the fire started by the bombing. Serov remained at our initial altitude of 6500 ft, while I climbed 3250 ft higher. My luck was in, for ten minutes later I spotted an enemy bomber heading towards me. He would not get away.

'Having let him pass, I turned and began to approach him at the same height from his right and behind. We had learned by then that the Junkers' fuel tank was positioned near the right wing root. Having approached the target and slowed down, I fired at that area. Flame appeared along the right side of the bomber's fuselage. Almost at once the enemy gunner responded, but he was too late. His bomber was already going down in flames. I followed him down almost to the

Maj Mikhail Yakushin poses alongside his I-16 Type 10 fighter on 18 August 1939 during Aviation Day celebrations – he was a member of an aerobatics team that displayed over Moscow on this date. Two years earlier Yakushin had claimed several victories in Spain flying I-15s with 1a/*Gruppo* 26. Indeed, on 26 July 1937 he had become the first Republican fighter pilot to shoot down a Ju 52/3m bomber at night. Yakushin's score included two individual and several shared victories

Anatoliy Serov fought in Spain from 14 June 1937 to 21 January 1938 as commander of I-15 squadron 1a/*Gruppo* 26. During this time he shot down eight enemy aircraft, including one destroyed at night. Serov was killed in a flying accident on 11 May 1939

ground. After that we left our patrol area a few minutes early and rushed home to spread the news of our victory. Once out of my cockpit and back on the ground I was immediately grabbed by Serov. He looked as triumphant as I was because our vertical split formation was his idea!'

Serov repeated this feat a few nights later when he too downed a Ju 52/3m – one of seven successes he would claim in July 1937. Anatoliy Serov had arrived in Spain on 14 June 1937, and he stayed until 21 January 1938. Having initially served as a squadron pilot in the Leningrad area, he subsequently became a test pilot in the mid-1930s, before volunteering for combat in Spain. Rising through the ranks, he led an I-15 squadron from August 1937 and was made group commander in mid-October following a successful strafing attack on Garapinilos airfield that resulted in a large number of Nationalist aircraft being destroyed. Serov's total flying time in Spain included 230+ combat hours, and he claimed eight individual and eight shared victories during the course of 48 engagements. Moreover, he personally removed a ninth victory from his record.

In recognition of his courage and bravery, Snr Lt Serov was honoured with the title of Hero of the Soviet Union on 2 March 1938. Later that year he was appointed Head of the Main Flight Inspection department of the VVS RKKA. He remained an active pilot as part of his new job, participating in the I-153 flight-testing programme and performing the leader's role in the I-16 'Red Five' aerobatic team. On 11 May 1939 brigade commander Serov died in a flying accident in a UTI-4 two-seater, together with the famous aviatrix Maj Polina Osipenko.

Mikhail Yakushin served in Spain from 31 May to 15 November 1937. His 180 flight hours included eight night sorties and 25 aerial engagements. His personal record shows three confirmed individual victories, as well as participation in several shared ones. Yakushin's performance in Spain was rewarded by two Orders of the Red Combat Banner. He continued to fly upon returning home, being a member of a five-aircraft aerobatic team. Yakushin was also appointed to a number of administrative posts, which did not help his advancement. By 1941 he was commanding the eastern sector of the Moscow Air Defence Forces.

Following the success enjoyed by Yakushin and Serov, night patrols by the I-15 group continued through to the end of 1937. Combat during daylight hours also increased in this period, with more Soviet pilots claiming their first victories. Patrols routinely intercepted Italian bombers making bombing raids on Barcelona from an airfield on Majorca. On the night of 25 October, after unsuccessfully firing at a three-engined SM.81 bomber of the 251st Squadron, ace Evgeniy Stepanov rammed the Savoia-Marchetti's tail with the propeller of his fighter. The Italian bomber crashed 2.5 miles from Barcelona, while Stepanov was able to bring his damaged I-15 safely home.

Having arrived in Spain in August 1937 after serving with 12th IAE of 111th IAB from the Leningrad Military District, Stepanov was posted to Serov's squadron. Engaged in combat operations from Los Alcazares, he is believed to have downed an estimated ten enemy aircraft, although many of his victories were never officially reported due to the pilot's reluctance to claim them. On 20 January 1938 Stepanov's I-15 was hit by anti-aircraft fire and he was forced to bail out. Quickly captured, he became a prisoner of war and was eventually exchanged for a captured enemy pilot. Returning to the USSR, Stepanov would later score additional victories during the Khalkhin Gol campaign and serve in various administrative positions within the VVS RKKA in World War 2.

During the Spanish Civil War the Soviet Union shipped a total of 131 I-15s to the Republicans, including 116 sent in 1936-37 to the central zone and 15 that arrived in early November 1936 in the northern zone. The Spanish and Soviet governments struck a deal in early 1937 that would see I-15 production commence in Spain, Polikarpov transferring the relevant technical documentation and engineering drawings in February. The first five Spanish-built I-15s were completed in August 1937 at the SAF-3 factory at Reus. By the end of 1938 a total of 213 *Chatos* had been built in Spain, with the last 24 being completed in January 1939 to take the total number of airframes (rather than complete aircraft) produced to 237 units. Of this total, some 96, built between November 1938 and January 1939, stood incomplete for lack of engines and other equipment. As a result, the total number of Soviet-made and locally built I-15s said to have participated in the Spanish Civil War varies between 272 and 368.

The exact number of I-15s lost during the campaign is also difficult to determine because the the Republicans destroyed a number of their own fighters while retreating. There is also a lack of reliable data on actual losses during the final stages of the war. By 1 January 1939, a total of 197 I-15s had reportedly been lost, including 88 shot down, 27 destroyed on the ground, 67 written off in accidents, nine downed by anti-aircraft artillery and six captured after force-landing in enemy territory. Yet Nationalist pilots (Spanish, Italian and German) reportedly claimed that about 500 I-15s had been shot down in air combat! Actual *Chato* losses were probably comparable to those of its principal rival, the CR.32. Of the 376 Fiat fighters shipped to Spain, 175 (43 Spanish-operated and 132 Italian) were lost, including 99 (26 Spanish and 73 Italian) shot down.

Evgeniy Antonov of 1a/*Gruppo* 26 poses in front of his I-15, tactical number 46, at Bajaralos, in Spain, in December 1937. In-theatre between 31 May 1937 and 28 January 1938, he commanded an I-15 squadron during this period. Logging 210 flying hours in Spain, Antonov shot down two enemy aircraft

Nikolay Shmelkov fought in Spain from 20 October 1936 to 23 January 1937, claiming five victories with the I-15 in 49 combat sorties. He then saw action in the Winter War in the I-16, before achieving more kills leading 145th IAP on the Karelian Front in the early weeks of the war in the east. Surviving the conflict, Shmelkov's final tally was 18 victories, most of which had been claimed with Polikarpov fighters

I-15 VICTORY LISTING

It is hard to judge exactly who were the most effective Soviet I-15 and I-16 pilots during the conflict in Spain because of the absence of data on personal scores, as well as the fact that victories were assigned to an entire squadron without individual attribution. In addition, the *pilotos rusos* often switched between I-15s and I-16s, making the compilation of statistics on enemy aircraft shot down even more complicated. Among the rare reliable historical documents is a cumulative victory roll dated 9 December 1936, which recorded the successes recorded by Pavel Rychagov's squadron up to that point in the war. Rychagov goes by the *nom de guerre* of 'Grinberg' in this document;

Document Name	Real Name	He 51	CR.32	'Fokker'	Ju 52/3m
Grinberg	Rychagov	3	2	-	1
Agafonov	Agafonov	2	-	-	-
Zakharov	Zakharov	0.5	0.5	1	-
Miroshninchenko	Miroshninchenko	0.5	0.5	-	-
Kazimir	Kovalesvskiy	1	-	-	-
Smelkov	Shmelkov*	3	0.5	-	-
Artemyev	Artemyev	1	0.5	-	-
Jose	Kopets	2	-	-	-
Pedro	Erlykin	0.5	-	-	-
Matyunin	Matyunin	2.5	-	-	-
Kombrat	Kondrat	0.5	-	-	-
Julio	Pumpar	-	-	-	2
Lacadie	Lacalle (Spanish)	1	-	-	-
Dary	D'Ary (French)	0.5	-	-	-

(*Data relating to Shmelkov was later corrected to show four personal victories and two shared)

A further indication of success among Soviet fighter pilots was nomination for the title of Hero of the Soviet Union. The Spanish campaign resulted in 34 aircrew (pilots, navigators and gunners) receiving the title. The following listing provides details of the I-15 pilots who were so honoured;

Name	Award Date	Comments
Karp Kovtun	31/12/36	Posthumous, as killed in action on 13/11/36
Pavel Rychagov	31/12/36	-
Nikolay Shmelkov	31/12/36	-
Boris Turzhanskiy	31/12/36	-
Ivan Kopets	21/6/37	Flew foreign fighter types as well as I-15
Petr Pumpar	4/7/37	Flew the I-16 too
Ivan Eremenko	28/10/37	-
Anatoliy Serov	2/3/38	-
Aleksander Osipenko	22/2/39	-

Some I-15 pilots involved in the campaign later received the title partly in recognition of their achievements in Spain. They included E Stepanov, E Erlykin, A Osadchiy, G Zakharov, V Kustov and E Kondrat.

ENTER THE I-16

The first I-16s appeared in Spanish skies to join the I-15s in November 1936, and they immediately acquired a local nickname – *Moska* could be interpreted as misspelled *Moscú* (Moscow) or, also misspelled, *Moshka* (Russian for blackfly). It was the latter interpretation which prevailed, although Soviet pilots initially applied different nicknames to the two fighters – the I-15 was called *Rak* (crawfish) and the I-16 *Shchuka* (pike). To the Nationalists, however, the I-16 became the *Rata* (Rat), a nickname that stuck. It was apparently derived from a remark made by a bomber crewman who was so impressed by the speed of the attacking I-16s that he commented 'they looked as if they were rats coming out of the drains!'

The first batch of 31 I-16 Type 5s was shipped from the USSR as part of a consignment of military aid supplied to the Spanish Republic. Accompanying the aircraft were 31 Soviet pilots, who arrived on 3 and 4 November aboard the transports *Kursk* and *Blagoev*. Led by Capt Sergey Tarkhov, they had been withdrawn from 83rd IAB of the Byelorussian Military District.

After assembly and flight-testing, some 16 I-16s left Alcantarilla on 8 November under Tarkhov's leadership and headed for Madrid.

Vladimir Bocharov's I-16 was captured near Madrid on 13 November 1936 when it was damaged during the type's very first action over Spain. The next day the Nationalists parachuted Bocharov's body into Madrid. It had been chopped up into pieces and packed in a box. The I-16, meanwhile, was repaired and thoroughly flight-tested

The unit, dubbed the *Grupo de Caza* by the Republicans, included *escuadrilla* headed by Vladimir Bocharov and Sergey Denisov. On the 10th the aircraft arrived safely at Alkalá de Henares airfield. The fighters were sent on their first patrol shortly after their arrival, flying sorties over the capital in support of Republican forces charged with clearing enemy troops out of the Casa de Campo Park area to the west of the city centre.

Three days later, 12 I-16s led by Tarkhov and a similar number of I-15s headed by Rychagov scrambled to intercept a Nationalist bombing raid on Madrid. The I-16s' first air combat also represented their Soviet pilots' baptism of fire. A complete lack of any combat experience was probably the main reason for their failure on this date, and the realities of the civil war proved to be difficult for the pilots to initially cope with. Group commander Sergey Tarkhov collided with an enemy aircraft and had to bail out, while Vladimir Bocharov's fighter was damaged so badly that he force-landed in enemy territory. He was immediately captured. The next day the Nationalists parachuted Bocharov's body into Madrid. It had been chopped up into pieces and packed in a box. As for Tarkhov, he was mistaken for an enemy pilot and shot as he descended in his parachute. Taken to hospital in Madrid, he died there a few days later.

But the enemy suffered too, the Republicans claiming four aerial victories. Two German He 51 pilots, Eberhardt and Henrizi, were indeed killed, the former perishing in a mid-air collision (possibly with Tarkhov) and the latter being shot down by future ace Sergey Chernykh.

On 14 November Andrey Morozov led 12 I-16s to Guadalajara airfield, near Madrid – two more fighters joined them a few days later, at which point Konstantin Kolesnikov assumed command of the group. The three units under his supervision were in turn led by Aleksander Negoreev, Sergey Denisov and Andrey Morozov. On the 15th nine I-16s took off to intercept Ju 52/3m bombers, escorted by fighters, heading for Madrid. Denisov and Chernykh each reported downing an enemy fighter. The latter pilot claimed his second victory on 13 December during a joint sortie with I-15s when he destroyed one of 18 newly deployed Heinkel He 70 monoplanes that were being used by the *Legion Condor* in the reconnaissance role. Chernykh got another Heinkel on 7 January 1937, as described by Georgiy Zakharov in his memoirs, although he mistook the He 70 for a Bf 109;

'Chernykh intercepted the Messerschmitt over our airfield. Everyone was surprised to see the fascist's reluctance to fight the lone I-16 – he just accelerated and tried to flee. However, fleeing also requires some skill and knowledge. Instead of remaining in level flight and taking advantage of his Messerschmitt's higher speed, its pilot showed a poor knowledge of the I-16's performance characteristics – or perhaps he was just scared stiff – and unexpectedly began to climb. It was his first fatal mistake.

'You shouldn't trifle with the I-16 in the climb. And he shouldn't have trifled with Chernykh either, for he was well known for his skill in fighting in a vertical plane. The I-16's powerful engine provided a much higher rate of climb, and Chernykh quickly caught the Messerschmitt. Then the German pilot made his second mistake. Sergey fired once he was in range, and missed. We felt disappointed. The fascist was given another chance to escape but he didn't take it. Instead, he stubbornly started climbing again. From his second approach Sergey fired again, but from closer range. The Messerschmitt disintegrated in mid-air, the debris hitting the ground near Alcala, where we went to take a look at it.'

Prior to heading to Spain, Sergey Chernykh had been commander of 107th IAE of 83rd IAB in the Byelorussian Military District, where he was widely acknowledged as being one of the best pilots in the VVS RKKA at that time. On 31 December 1936 he had been among the first pilots to receive the title of Hero of the Soviet Union, and by February 1937, after nearly three months in Spain, Chernykh had flown almost 112 combat flying hours and claimed five individual and two shared victories.

Following his return from Spain, Chernykh continued his military service, and in June 1941 he commanded 9th SAD (*Smeshannaya Aviatsionniy Diviziya* – Combined Air Division) of the Western Military District. During the German onslaught on 22 June 1941, 9th SAD lost 347 of its 409 aircraft. As divisional commander Chernykh was held responsible for these catastrophic losses by Stalin, and he was executed on 26 June alongside other commanders blamed for the VVS RKKA's disastrous showing during the opening days of the Great Patriotic War.

Among the first group of Soviet pilots to see combat in the I-16 in Spain, the most successful were group commander Kolesnikov and pilots Lakeev, Minaev and Denisov. The latter, who had joined the Red Army in 1929, eventually replaced Kolesnikov as unit commander, and he

Soviet-built I-16 Type 10 CM-225 was assigned to 7 *Escuadrilla/Grupo de Caza* in 1937. A number of volunteer pilots flew this aircraft in combat

remained in Spain until April 1937. By the time he returned to the USSR, Denisov had flown nearly 200 sorties and claimed 12 personal and two shared victories. However, documents from the period show that his achievements were actually a far more modest three individual and two shared victories, although his combat proficiency was beyond doubt.

On 4 April 1937 Denisov was awarded the title of Hero of the Soviet Union. Two years later he participated in the Khalkhin Gol campaign, and during the Soviet-Finnish war he commanded the 7th Army Air Force. In 1940 Denisov was again awarded the title of Hero of the Soviet Union, and he held positions of senior command in World War 2.

TAKING STOCK

A relative lull in the action in the third week of November 1936 furnished *Grupo de Caza* with the opportunity to take stock after giving the I-16 its combat debut in Spain. The unit had lost four fighters to date, with one undergoing repair. Such attrition led to the Republican air force reluctantly acknowledging that the monoplane's higher speed might not necessarily lead to dominance of the enemy's biplane fighters in the skies over Spain. Success in combat situations required pilots to develop flying skills that were tempered with caution and enhanced by guile. Overconfidence and hasty actions could be harmful, if not fatal. But experience was soon acquired and the I-16 detachment suffered no losses in December. By the end of the year the newly arrived fighter pilots had achieved 15 aerial victories in just two months.

In January 1937 their ranks were reinforced by a further group of Soviet pilots. This new blood would eventually replace the original cadre of experienced aviators sent to Spain in early November 1936. Their arrival coincided with an extended period of poor weather that reduced flying to just a few combat sorties well into February. However, that all changed mid-month when a series of major air combats was fought on 12, 14 and 18 February over the central sector of the frontline. The clashes clearly demonstrated the I-16's superiority, as pilots made full use of their growing proficiency to claim more than ten enemy aircraft destroyed. These successes did not come without a price, and on 18 February, for example, Filipp Zamashanskiy was badly wounded when he crashed while attempting to force-land a shot-up I-16 away from his airfield.

Between 14 and 28 March there were 17 combat-ready I-16s in the central front and seven under repair. Six had been lost in combat and one destroyed in an accident. Pilot numbers remained the same a month later, but in May 59 more arrived from the USSR, accompanied by 60 Spanish graduates from the Soviet flying school at Kirovabad.

At the same time 62 new I-16 Type 5s were delivered from the USSR to bolster the Republican air force, but these new fighters quickly proved to be far from combat-ready. Their M-25A engines demonstrated poor quality control and their wings lacked proper strengthening. A series of fatal accidents ensued, causing a loss of confidence in the aircraft. Soviet representatives in Spain even went as far as to label the new batch of fighters the 'sabotaged aircraft' in the reports they sent back to Moscow. Their investigations into the crashes indicated that pilots Lesnikov, Moseyko, Burov and Orzhanov has been killed when their fighters suffered wing failure in flight.

All remaining I-16s from this batch were subjected to improvements in the field, including the strengthening and replacement of the fabric skin on the outer wing panels. Before this could happen, however, Konstantin Kolesnikov was killed when the wings of his I-16 folded up in mid-air on 12 May 1937. He had four personal and three shared victories to his credit at the time of his death, and on 4 July Kolesnikov was posthumously awarded the title of Hero of the Soviet Union.

In June-July 1937 new fighter units designated as squadrons were formed, and by year-end five had been established under the command of Ivan Lakeev, Anton Moseyko, Valentin Ukhov, Aleksander Minaev and Grigoriy Pleshchenko.

A handful of American pilots journeyed to Spain as 'soldiers of fortune' in 1936, and by far the most successful were Frank Tinker, Albert 'Ajax' Baumler and Harold 'Whitey' Dahl. An ex-US Naval Aviator, Tinker had had his commission revoked in 1935 due to disciplinary problems, and he eventually travelled to Spain in late 1936 under the *nom de guerre* 'Francisco Gomez Trejo'. The latter was done to avoid him falling foul of the US government's non-intervention policy in respect to the Spanish Civil War. Hastily checked out in the I-15, Tinker flew his first sortie on 7 January 1937 and claimed two CR.32s and a He 51 destroyed in March and April while assigned to the squadron led by Andre Garcia Lacalle. He transferred to Ivan Lakeev's squadron in early May upon his conversion to the I-16, and Tinker would claim an additional three CR.32s and two Bf 109s destroyed between 2 June and 18 July. He was paid compensation totalling $18,500 for his exploits in Spain, and returned home in late August. Tinker committed suicide on 13 June 1939.

Baumler was unsuccessful in his attempt to fly fighters with the US Army Air Corps (USAAC), being eliminated from training in June 1936. Receiving a commercial transport rating four months later, he had made his way to Spain by late 1936. Checked out in the I-15 in February 1937, Baumler was also assigned to Lacalle's squadron. Between 16 March and 17 April he claimed one and one shared CR.32s destroyed, one He 51 shot down and a second Heinkel fighter as a probable. Converting to the I-16 in late May, Baumler claimed two more CR.32s destroyed and a third one as a probable prior to returning home in August. Commissioned into the USAAC, he saw more action flying P-40Es in China in 1942-43, initially on attachment to the American Volunteer Group and then with the 23rd Fighter Group (FG). Indeed, Baumler claimed a further 4.5 kills in action against the Japanese Army Air Force (JAAF) in 1942, and became CO of the 23rd FG's 74th Fighter Squadron the following year.

Like Tinker, 'Whitey' Dahl was forced to resign his commission (from the USAAC) in February 1936 due to a series of misdemeanours. Volunteering for service with the Republican air force in early 1937, Dahl adopted the *nom de guerre* 'Hernando Diaz Evans' and joined Lacalle's I-15 squadron in February. After claiming a handful of victories over He 51s and CR.32s, Dahl converted to the I-16 in the spring and was shot down and taken prisoner on 13 July. By then he had claimed five biplane kills. Remaining in prison until 1940, he returned to the USA and joined the Royal Canadian Air Force in 1941. After seeing further action, Dahl became a civilian pilot in the 1950s and perished when his DC-3 crashed in Quebec, Canada, on 14 February 1956.

Three French pilots also claimed kills in the I-15 and I-16, Abel Guides being credited with ten victories prior to his death in combat on 6 August 1937. A pilot by the name of Rayneau claimed five, as did William Laboussiére, who was CO of the I-16-equipped 1 *Escuadrilla* in 1937. Returning to France the following year with five

Having had their Republican markings removed, these captured I-16s were photographed in Spain in the summer of 1939

victories to his name, he saw further action (and claimed more kills) in China in 1939 and with the *Armée de l'Air* in Indochina in World War 2.

There were at least 17 Spanish pilots who 'made ace' during the civil war, and most of them scored the bulk of their victories in the I-15 and/or I-16. A future volume in this series will detail their combat experiences.

In early July 1937 the first Spanish I-16 squadron was formed, initially under the command of future ace Boris Smirnov. Snr Lt Smirnov had arrived in Spain the previous month, and he flew missions through to January 1938. As an I-16 pilot he downed two aircraft in Spain, while his squadron reported scoring 16 victories. Smirnov would later serve in the Khalkhin Gol conflict as an instructor with 70th IAP (*Istrebitelniy Aviatsionniy Polk* – Fighter Aviation Regiment), with whom he would shoot down four aircraft in nine aerial engagements. On 17 November 1939 Smirnov was awarded the title of Hero of the Soviet Union.

In July 1937 the Republicans began an offensive at Brunete with the objective of encircling enemy forces near Madrid. They had 50+ combat-ready I-15s and I-16s at their disposal, but the Nationalists could put up more than 140 fighters, including nine of the newest Bf 109Bs. This gave them overwhelming quantitative superiority, which was the primary cause of the heavy combat losses suffered by the Republicans throughout the year. Despite reinforcement, the number of operational I-16s in the central sector of the front had fallen to 30 by the end of July. The number of *Moskas* lost in air combat since autumn 1936 had reached 25.

On 12 July a huge dogfight took place near El Escorial when 29 I-16s from the squadrons commanded by Lakeev, Vinogradov and Shevtsov, together with eight I-15s of Eremenko's unit, attacked a group of 40 He 51s and CR.32s. Both sides initially claimed nine victories each, although both only admitted losing one fighter. A few hours later a squadron of Polikarpov R-Z biplane reconnaissance bombers was attacked by what the surviving crews described as 'high-speed monoplanes', but were probably Bf 109Bs, although they were not yet identified as such. Escorting I-16s attempted to engage the aircraft in what was probably the first engagement between the *Moska* and the new German fighter. The I-16s suffered no losses, but the Bf 109B of Gustav Hoeness was shot down. The victory was attributed to a number of Soviet pilots, but the author believes that it was achieved by Petr Burtym.

On 17 and 18 July two more Bf 109Bs went down, one of which probably fell victim to I-16 pilot Frank Tinker. Claims for shooting down Messerschmitt fighters would regularly appear in pilots' reports in coming months, although wreckage was rarely found to support these victories. However, the Republicans were able to capture a Bf 109B in

This Bf 109B of *Legion Condor* unit 1.J/88 was captured after its pilot, Unteroffizier Otto Polenz, was forced to land the fighter behind Republican lines at Corta Azaila-Escatron, on the Aragon front, with a damaged fuel system on 4 December 1937. The German fighter was one of 11 Bf 109Bs escorting 30 Nationalist bombers that were engaged by five I-16s led by Aleksander Gusev. Polenz's aircraft was subsequently evaluated by a French team from the *Armée de l'Air*, prior to it being shipped to the USSR. Gusev would claim four and one shared victories in Spain, and he subsequently saw action in Mongolia and during World War 2, although he claimed no more victories

almost serviceable condition on 4 December 1937 when five I-16s led by ace Aleksander Gusev encountered some 30 Nationalist bombers escorted by 11 Bf 109s of 1.J/88. A Bf 109B was shot down in Nationalist-held territory, and a second one was forced to land behind Republican lines with a damaged fuel system. Gusev and his wingman escorted it down and then circled overhead until friendly troops arrived to take possession of the Messerschmitt, and pilot Unteroffizier Otto Polenz. The aircraft was subsequently evaluated by a team from the *Armée de l'Air*, prior to being shipped to the USSR.

Gusev recalled the desperate combats of late 1937 that saw I-16 pilots struggling to survive in the air against both German and Italian fighters;

'We fought the Fiats at the limit of our abilities throughout 1937. On one occasion in the autumn I saw three Fiats attacking my squadronmate Platon Smolyakov in the distance. Having dropped out of the dogfight, he risked becoming easy prey, and although I was too far from him to come to his rescue, Ivan Devotchenko's squadron went to his aid. I later discovered that the pilot who saved Smolyakov was future high-scoring ace Lev Shestakov. Having seen that one of the Fiats was going to open fire on Smolyakov, Lev drove his aircraft in between them and took a lot of the fire himself. He was lucky to avoid being hurt, but his I-16 was holed in a dozen places. Two bullets hit the armoured backplate and another ripped open the leather pants he was so proud of! Having covered Smolyakov, Devotchenko's unit downed one of the Fiats.'

In an effort to redress the growing imbalance in both quality and quantity between the Republican and Nationalist air arms, in April 1938 the USSR sent 31 I-16 Type 10s powered by M-25V engines to Spain, but again they proved to be of substandard quality when uncrated on their arrival. This was confirmed by a new crop of Soviet pilots who flight-tested the aircraft and then reported several alarming faults. Defects in the construction of the engines, as well as unsafe armament, caused a general reluctance among pilots to fly combat missions in the new fighters. As a result, on 21 May 1938 there were just 43 combat-ready *Moska*s in Spain.

Aside from the two Soviet units (2nd and 5th) equipped with the aircraft, there were three Spanish squadrons too, the 1st, 3rd and 4th. Early in August 1938 the Republicans received 90 improved I-16 Type 10 fighters, which enabled additional squadrons to be formed. At the same time new fighter aces emerged, including Sergey Gritsevets.

During his service in Spain, from 10 June to 26 October 1938, when all volunteer pilots were recalled to the USSR, Gritsevets commanded 5 *Escuadrilla de Caza* and then the whole group of I-16s. Having claimed a single kill over a Japanese aircraft attacking Hangchow on 29 April 1938, Gritsevets then volunteered for combat in Spain. Here he flew 88 sorties and fought in 42 aerial battles, and according to legend he shot down no fewer than 30 enemy aircraft. However, this tally probably reflects the total claimed by the unit whilst under his command because Gritsevets always stressed that enemy aircraft shot down should be

31

credited to the unit as a whole, rather than to the individual. Nevertheless, official reports credit him with seven personal aerial victories in Spain.

In any case, Snr Lt Gritsevets was judged to be a distinguished fighter pilot, and on 22 February 1939 he was awarded the title of Hero of the Soviet Union. That summer he became a squadron commander with 70th IAP and participated in the Khalkhin Gol campaign, where he increased his personal score by 12 more kills. On 23 August Gritsevets performed the heroic act of landing his I-16 on the steppe amid enemy troops to rescue his CO, Maj V Zabaluev, who had been forced to bail out 60 kilometres behind Japanese lines. Six days later Sergey Gritsevets was again honoured with the Hero of the Soviet Union Star, but he was killed in a flying accident at Bolbasovo airfield on 16 September 1939.

Mikhail Fedoseev was almost as successful as Gritsevets, and like the latter he too had arrived in Spain in late June 1938 with a group of specially selected pilots. Prior to that he had served as a flight commander with 4th IAE of 56th IAB, Kiev Military District. Fedoseev's first aerial combat came during the bitter fighting over the Ebro River, and from then until his departure in November 1938 he engaged the enemy 40 times and downed five aircraft. On his return from Spain Fedoseev was made CO of 6th OIAE (*Otdelnaya Aviatsionniy Eskadrilya* – Independent Fighter Aviation Squadron) and then promoted to the position of deputy commander of 88th IAP. In World War 2 he led 247th IAP and downed 20 aircraft, but he was himself killed in action on 23 March 1942. Fedoseev posthumously received the title of Hero of the Soviet Union.

Another leading I-16 ace in Spain was Vladimir Bobrov, who joined the Republicans in March 1938. Having previously served with 57th IAE of 142nd IAB, Byelorussian Military District, by the time he left Spain in the autumn he had flown 78 sorties in the I-16, participated in eight aerial combats and brought down four aircraft, with 13 more shared.

On the first day of the war with Germany Bobrov destroyed an He 111, but he was himself shot down soon afterwards, receiving severe burns that necessitated long and extensive treatment in hospital. In April 1943 he was made CO of 27th IAP, and flew the LaGG-3, Yak-1 and P-39. On 11 August 1944, then commander of 104th GIAP Lt Col Bobrov was nominated for the title Hero of the Soviet Union, although he would not actually receive it until 1991. By the end of World War 2, Bobrov had completed an impressive 577 combat sorties, participated in 159 aerial combats and officially scored 30 personal and 20 shared kills.

The total number of Polikarpov monoplanes shipped to Spain in 1936-38 amounted to 276 I-16s and four UTI-4 trainers. Monthly shipments were as follows – 31 I-16s in October 1936, 62 I-16s and four UTI-4s in May 1937, 62 I-16s in August 1937, 31 I-16s in March 1938 and 90 I-16s in August of that same year. Within three months of the last examples having been delivered to the Republicans, all Soviet pilots had been withdrawn from Spain on direct orders from the Kremlin and returned to the USSR. A total of 160 Soviet fighter pilots had seen action in the conflict, with 35 being created Heroes of the Soviet Union.

The war ended on 1 April 1939 following the surrender of Republican forces. By then some 187 I-16s had been lost in Spain, with 112 downed in combat, one claimed by anti-aircraft fire, 11 destroyed on the ground, 62 lost in accidents and one force-landed in enemy-held territory.

HSU's CHINA 1937-39

ANTON GUBENKO   7/3/39 KIRR

Col Aleksey BLAGOVESHCHENSKY 14/11/38 13
                                        3/3/3

PETR KOVCHENKO   1 MAY1943 13 13 ILS

KONSTANTIN KOKKINAKI   21/8 1964

charges' section below.

Item	Payee	Amount (GBP)
D/D	NATWEST LOAN	63.14

We'll send you itemised details of any Returned Item Fees on a 'Pre-advice Notice' which will normally come with your statement. The charges will be taken from your account 21 days after the end of the charging period in which we decide not to make the payment (or on the next business day if this is a Saturday, Sunday, or bank holiday). The charging period normally ends on the date that we send your statement to you. We will always let you know how much we are going to take and when we will take it, in advance.

We don't charge Returned Item Fees on savings accounts.

What to do next

There are a few things you should do:

- Check your balance and pay money in to your account to cover any future payments. This will help prevent you getting further charges.
- Tell the person or organisation expecting your payment that it has not been made.
- Remember that if a standing order or Direct Debit on your account is unpaid more than once and we reasonably think that the cleared balance (or any unused arranged overdraft) is unlikely to be enough to meet future payments we may cancel it.

LUP001

National Westminster Bank Plc. Registered in England and Wales No. 929027. Registered Office: 135 Bishopsgate, London EC2M 3UR. Authorised and regulated by the Financial Services Authority. VAT Registration No. GB 243-8527-52. Calls may be recorded.

RBS

SWALLOWS OVER CHINA

Shipments of I-15 and I-16 fighters from the Soviet Union to China commenced in the autumn of 1937 as part of a programme of military aid to assist the Chinese Air Force (CAF) of the Kuomintang Government in its defensive war against the Japanese Army Air Force (JAAF) and the Imperial Japanese Naval Air Force (IJNAF).

Initially, the CAF had relied on US combat aircraft such as the Curtiss Hawk III biplane fighter. However, when simmering tensions in China erupted in July 1937, the CAF's early engagements with IJNAF A5M2 'Claude' fighters quickly revealed just how obsolete these American machines were. The following month the Chinese government hastily signed a non-aggression pact with the USSR, which quickly resulted in 255 I-15s being hastily supplied to the CAF, along with more than 250 volunteer pilots to fly them. Soviet support for the Chinese would remain secret, the undertaking being codenamed Operation *Zet*.

These fighters were the first of 885 Soviet aircraft supplied to the Chinese between October 1937 and September 1939, the bulk of these being fighters in the following quantities – 216 I-16 Type 5s and 10s, 347 I-15/I-15bis and about 100 I-153s. By 1941 the total number of Soviet aircraft shipped to China reached 1250 of various types.

Most of the aircraft intended for the CAF were assembled at Alma-Ata, with the first examples sent being ferried to Lanzhou – a formidable 1500-mile journey over the Tien Shan mountain range and the deserts of northeastern China. Such an undertaking represented an unprecedented venture for the Soviet pilots involved, as they endured poor visibility and dust storms when landing at various hastily prepared airfields located deep within mountain ravines. To reduce the risk, further batches of fighters were transported overland on ZIS-5 trucks to the northern Chinese airfield of Hami from early 1938. There, the aircraft were assembled and flight-tested, before heading over the desert to Lanzhou.

Clearly bearing the Chinese Kuomintang 12-ray star insignia beneath their wings, as well as the CAF's blue and white rudder stripes, these I-16s were photographed at an unprepared airfield near Nanjing in 1938

Once at the latter airfield, the Kuomintang 12-ray star insignia was applied to the aircraft, which were now deemed to have been transferred to the CAF. From then on the Soviet pilots flying these machines would wear red silk strips onto which a message had been written instructing locals to give them any assistance they needed in case of a forced landing.

Some publications suggest that the first batch of 62 fighters delivered to China in November-December 1937 comprised I-15s, rather than the new I-15bis, although the available documents neither support nor rebut that version of events. Logically, the supply of the I-15bis to China in the autumn of that year seems unlikely because, officially, the first fighters of that type were not accepted from the manufacturer until early 1938. On the other hand, the fate of about 100 I-15bis built by Factory No 1 in the second half of 1937 is still not clear, as there is no information pertaining to where they were delivered. The suggestion that the first batch of I-15s delivered to China included at least some I-15bis is therefore credible. And in none of the memoirs of the actual participants in these events is there any reference to 'regular' I-15s being used in China, as only the improved 'bis' variant is mentioned.

I-16s began arriving in China at this time too. In the second half of September the first group of 23 fighters, led by Gennadiy Prokifyev, crossed Chinese territory from west to east. Documents show that eight I-16s flown by Soviet pilots landed at their final destination – the airfield near Nanjing. Some were transferred to Chinese pilots of the 4th Pursuit Group (PG) in Hangchow, but the hurried training programme that had been instigated by the CAF was insufficient to enable these novice aviators to master such a demanding fighter. A large number of I-16s were written off in accidents as a result.

On 1 December Prokifyev's group flew its first patrol in the area around Nanjing, which had become the Chinese capital after Shanghai fell to the Japanese on 11 November. During the course of the mission, the seven Soviet I-16 pilots involved claimed to have downed two enemy bombers and a fighter without loss from a group of 20 targeting Nanjing.

New nicknames were now bestowed on the Soviet fighters at this point, although their actual origin remains obscure. The I-16 became the *Lastochka* ('Swallow'), while the I-15bis was known as the *Chizh* ('Siskin'). Later, the Japanese would apply their own nickname to the Soviet monoplane, the I-16 becoming known as *Aboo* ('Gadfly') to JAAF and IJNAF pilots alike. Indeed, the fighter soon proved to be as quick and evasive as a gadfly upon its introduction to combat over China.

In early December 1937 additional Soviet pilots arrived to bolster the air defence of Nanjing, including future ace Dmitriy Kudymov. At this early stage of the war the Nanjing air group comprised about 30 fighters of different types, although the Soviet pilots exclusively flew Polikarpovs. Chinese I-15bis and I-16 pilots were also participating in air combats, and Kudymov recalled that things did not go quite to plan during his unit's introduction to the air war in China;

'Our first air combat could hardly be classified as a complete success, for we lost Andreev, while Remizov ran into a bomb crater and was killed on landing. However, our tally of victories offset these losses – we had destroyed six enemy LB-92 bombers (light bomber Type 92s in Soviet classification, these aircraft actually being IJNAF Yokosuka B4Y1 biplanes). A total of about 20 Japanese bombers participated in that raid, escorted by I-96 fighters (interceptor Type 96, which was the IJNAF Mitsubishi A5M2 monoplane fighter). The CAF had not seen this type over Nanjing up until now, having been driven from the skies over Shanghai by it earlier in the year when flying the Hawk III. We had studied the I-96 back in the Soviet Union, however, and we knew that it was inferior to our "Swallows" in every way.

'The Chinese pilots had only a vague knowledge of the I-96, which some believed was then the best fighter in the world. "Fear has big eyes", I thought, and my colleague Zhukotskiy shared my opinion. The Chinese pilots had suffered steady losses in aerial combat up until now, yet we still had to take off four or five times a day because the Japanese bombers approached the city in wave after wave, and they had a numerical advantage. On the other hand, I should pay tribute to the Chinese pilots for their courage. They were daring and performed to the best of their ability. But combat is combat, and you cannot win with bravery alone.

'The training received by the Chinese pilots was obviously insufficient, particularly in comparison with the highly trained Japanese pilots they were up against. Moreover, the latter also demonstrated great courage in air combat. And I can confirm this from my own experience of meeting a so-called "king of the sky". He was one of the top four aces of the IJNAF. They had been dubbed both "the invincibles" and "the lords of the sky". Before combat sorties we would see Chinese pilots praying that they wouldn't meet one of them while they were aloft.

'One morning our unit stood ready for immediate take-off. We waited in our cockpits, already hot from the merciless sun. The enemy didn't usually appear that early. The Japanese bombers tended to arrive by midday. Suddenly, I heard my Chinese mechanic shrieking, *Japan! Japan theitsi!* ("Japanese aircraft!"). Peering in the direction he was pointing, I saw in the white-hot sky a tiny black spot rapidly approaching the airfield. The enemy? It was doubtful, as Japanese pilots didn't usually behave like that. Then a thought flashed through my mind – could it be my luck to fight a one-on-one duel?

'The mechanic was already spinning up the propeller. I couldn't wait for the red flare signal to take-off for they were usually late – the air raid warning system at Nanjing performed poorly, and we often took off when the enemy had already reached the city or even the airfield. So I just took off. It was the right decision.

'While I was climbing, before levelling off and retracting the landing gear with 42 turns of the handle, the enemy fighter had already approached the airfield and was diving on me. I thought he was coming down on me like a hawk on a quail. I dropped the gear handle, applied full throttle and turned to meet the Japanese fighter nose-to-nose in a head-on attack! Too late. The enemy had already fired a burst from about 300 metres, and I felt my aircraft jolt. He dived steeply beneath me and then abruptly swerved upwards. It was clear that he was going to attack me from behind, so I immediately levelled my aircraft off and resumed turning the gear handle. Staying calm was the key.

'The Japanese pilot had not yet completed his turn, so I had a few seconds before he opened fire. And then, hurrah, my aircraft rushed forward like a racehorse – the landing gear was retracted at last! I headed for the enemy but the g-forces almost blinded me. Condensation swirled from my wingtips. During another sharp turn I noticed the wing skin swelling and shrinking like an accordion. And then I saw a series of red lightning stripes before me and the blood red insignia on the wings of my enemy. We were circling in a bizarre merry-go-round. The I-96 was madly buzzing in front of me, so dexterous and so elusive.

'Today it's difficult to remember every detail of that duel. At the time it seemed to last an eternity, but it was probably all over in about ten minutes. I suppose the Japanese ace couldn't stand the g-forces any longer and decided to dive away, so when I moved upwards he desperately entered an inside loop with the intention of escaping. At this point I must have been driven by my "fighter instinct". I abruptly abandoned my turn and dived just in time to fire a long burst into the belly of the I-96.

'He crashed at the edge of the airfield. The Chinese pilots were the first to meet me, congratulating me with enthusiastic cheers. My formation leader Tung excitedly explained the meaning of the arrows and other symbols displayed on the fuselage of my trophy – I had just downed a "king of the sky". Later, in February 1938, after our re-deployment to Nanchang, the Chief Soviet Military Adviser at Chiang Kai-shek's HQ, Divisional Commander Mikhail Dratvin, revealed the names of the two "kings" I had by then shot down. I have forgotten them now, of course.'

In January 1938 the Soviet fighters were redeployed to Nanchang, and the I-16 detachment was put under the command of future ace Alexei Blagoveshchenskiy. The pilots' workload was extremely high during this period, as Dmitriy Kudymov recalled;

'We took off two or three times a day to repulse the enemy raids. Death was always around, although it kept missing us. And this wasn't just due to luck, because we'd accumulated a lot of practical experience by then. Fighting in the dive had become our preferred technique because neither the Japanese aircraft or their pilots could take it for any prolonged period of time. We had learned to take advantage of the higher speed and better manoeuvrability of our "Swallows" too. But our resources were limited – fatigue degraded the metal parts of our aircraft, as well as our nerves and muscles. As for me, my body weight had dropped to little more than 50 kg. I had completely lost my appetite, and not just because of the poor food. Other Soviet volunteer pilots felt the same, and we were all exhausted from the near constant aerial combat.

'Clearly sensing that our spirits were at a low ebb, Divisional Commander Mikhail Dratvin travelled to Nanchang and visited us at the airfield. He gathered all the Soviet volunteers together and delivered the following address;

'"It's hard boys isn't it? Yes, it is, and I can see that for myself. I'm not going to soothe you with Chiang Kai-shek's recent praise, however. He told me that the Chinese pilots had clearly learned to fight more effectively following your arrival.

A total of 347 I-15s and I-15bis (examples of which are seen here) were supplied to the Chinese between October 1937 and September 1939, and both variants enjoyed notable success against Japanese aircraft during the conflict

Yes, that is indeed true, but some people in the CAF are obviously abusing your courage by repeatedly sending the Soviet volunteers into the most keenly contested areas to engage the enemy.'"

'We were all boiling mad because the other foreign volunteers – the pilots of the Gladiators, Hawk IIIs and Fiats – would never engage in a combat first, preferring to wait for the Soviet pilots to "pull their chestnuts out of the fire". Yet they'd claim to have shot down the enemy aircraft that we'd accounted for. "Goods (i.e. victories) shouldn't be lost. Isn't that your Russian saying?" smiled the interpreter. "You reject fees and prefer to risk your lives for an ideal rather than for dollars. That's what you're told to do, isn't it?"'

One of Kudymov's most successful actions took place on 18 February 1938 when the Soviet volunteers fought alongside the I-15bis and I-16s of the 4th PG in the dogged defence of Wuhan. Attacking a formation of 15 G3M 'Nell' bombers escorted by 11 A5M 'Claude' fighters at 1000 hrs, the Soviet pilots claimed 12 victories for the loss of three aircraft. I-16 aces Kudymov and Blagoveshchenskiy were each credited with an A5M destroyed, as was I-15bis ace Georgiy Zakharov.

The latter pilot had already enjoyed success in Spain, having returned to the USSR with six individual and four shared victories to his name, for which he was twice awarded the Order of Combat Red Banner. On his return to the Soviet Union, Zakharov was promoted to captain, participated in I-15bis testing and was then posted to China in late 1937, where he flew combat missions and acted as a fighter tactics instructor.

Zakharov's first victory for the CAF took the form of an A5M that landed intact following the 18 February 1938 clash over Wuhan – fellow pilot Aleksey Dushin also claimed a shared in the aircraft too. Zakharov described this episode in his memoirs;

'During the air engagement an I-96 suddenly began descending, although it appeared to have suffered no visible damage. I judged that the enemy pilot might be wounded. I kept a close eye on him, and soon it was clear that he was going to land, so I followed him down. This action happened over the flat steppe, so there was no difficulty in him landing. Aside from myself and the Japanese pilot, a second I-16 flown by a Mongolian by the name of Tun also landed nearby.

'As we approached the Japanese aircraft we heard a gun shot – the pilot had committed suicide. Then we smelled smoke and saw it seeping from the cockpit. I climbed up onto the wing and saw that the smoke was coming from burning maps and documents, the latter being a record of the missions flown and lists of active and dead pilots. The Japanese pilot (possibly Lt Takashi Kaneko) had apparently been commander of a fighter unit. We inspected the aircraft and soon determined the reason for the forced landing – the engine had been damaged, but in all other respects the fighter was completely untouched. We had captured a Japanese fighter, which was now made available for thorough inspection.'

After several test flights Zakharov was ordered to fly the A5M back to the USSR – by then he had downed a second 'Claude' in combat. Ahead of him lay a hazardous journey over several thousand kilometres. He subsequently recalled;

'For three days I was kept on the ground as the weather along the route was terrible. When I was finally allowed to take-off, it turned out that

Seen here while commanding 303rd IAD on the Kursk Front in 1943, Lt Gen Georgiy Zakharov was a veteran of the wars in Spain and China. Having claimed six individual and four shared victories flying the I-15 in Spain in 1936-37, he was credited with three more kills in China in 1938. Zakharov achieved a further nine victories in the I-16 during World War 2

some of my personal belongings had been stolen from the cockpit. All I had with me was what could be fitted into the cockpit, so I had left it there. Now I had nothing left apart from a tiny toy gun – a gift from my Chinese commander, which was in my hip-pocket.

'Of course, I was worried about the intrusion in the cockpit of my aircraft. Our official representative was also concerned about it. The Chinese guard was immediately interrogated, and he reported that many people had visited the aeroplane, taken off the covers, taken photographs and generally interfered with it. After that the guard mysteriously disappeared from the base. We thoroughly inspected the aircraft for any evidence of sabotage but found nothing suspicious, so I took off for Xi'an. On the way I landed in Xianyang to refuel. I again took off immediately, not trusting the people there either.

'The Xianyang to Xi'an leg was probably the hardest of the whole trip, so I was eager to get on with it as soon as possible. The flight was just within the fighter's maximum range. Secondly, I had to cross mountains with no emergency airfield available if I had to land. I cruised at an altitude of 13,000 ft.

'The entire itinerary had been agreed prior to my departure, and I was under close surveillance. I had to report to Moscow as soon as I arrived at the intermediate points in the journey. An hour after taking off from Xianyang the engine failed. It just coughed twice and stopped, leaving the propeller blades horizontal – they seemed like whiskers mocking me. The aircraft was going down fast, but I couldn't bail out because I couldn't see the ground. In any case, it was my duty to save this aircraft that had been captured after so much hard effort.

'Soon I entered thick clouds, hoping that they would not go all the way down to the ground. Yet here I was going down and down but still in thick cloud. It seemed like a disaster in the making, with a mountain range somewhere down there. It was sheer chance that took me out of the clouds in between two steep hills. I was flying along a ravine, and there was a shallow river, or rather a creek, below. As the ravine ended the creek widened into a waterfall. I had neither height nor time left for any deliberation, so I just turned the aeroplane and decided to land it right onto the stones of the waterfall. The last thing I remember before the crash-landing was trying to ward off the inevitable blow by stretching out my left arm and pressing my hand against the instrument panel.'

Zakharov broke his left arm in the crash-landing. A rescue team found him three days later and took him to Lanzhou for transfer to Moscow aboard a DB-3 bomber. During the summer of 1938, the Peoples' Commissariat of Defence issued an Order, dated 16 July, promoting Zakharov to the rank of colonel.

As previously mentioned, the ace's final victory in China had come on 29 April 1938, when Soviet volunteers in 23 I-15bis and 16 I-16s engaged 23 G3M2s and 27 A5Ms that had targeted Wuhan. Aleksey Dushin was flying one of the I-15bis, and he recalled in his memoirs that the Soviet pilots took off early, with the first flight being led away by Aleksey Blagoveshchenskiy, followed by the rest of the group. The I-15bis were to tackle the Japanese fighters while the I-16s went after the bombers.

Having received plenty of warning of the enemy attack, the Soviet fighters climbed away from their base at Hankou and headed in the direction of Nanking, from where the enemy formation had originated. Failing to spot the A5Ms, the I-15bis turned around and headed back to Wuhan. It was at this point that the pilots spotted a large group of bombers approaching on a parallel course through gaps in the clouds. Diving on the G3M2s, they attacked from close range and set three of the bombers alight, including the lead aircraft. The formation fell apart and jettisoned its bombs in a rice paddy. IJNAF fighters now also appeared on the scene, and a series of dogfights broke out that lasted 30 minutes. By the time the action ended, the CAF pilots had claimed 11 fighters and 10 bombers shot down – the largest single mission haul of the air war in China. Two Soviet and three Chinese pilots were killed in return.

A number of pilots made claims, including future ranking Soviet ace in China Grigoriy Kravchenko, who was credited with destroying both a bomber and a fighter. He then got separated from his wingman and was targeted by four A5Ms, who set his aircraft on fire. Kravchenko was saved from certain death by future ace Anton Gubenko, who managed to fend off his Japanese attackers and claim his first kill. Aces Aleksey Blagoveshchenskiy and Sergey Gritsevets also claimed single victories.

The Russian pilots credited their success to the fact that the A5Ms had arrived late at the rendezvous point with the bombers. The volunteers had also made successful use of the cloud cover to mask their approach.

Having opened his account on 29 April, Spanish Civil War veteran Anton Gubenko would go on to score a further six kills between then and 18 July – the first four were claimed in the I-15bis and the remaining three in an I-16. Fighting with the CAF from March to August 1938, Gubenko rammed an I-96 with his I-15bis during an air battle near Hankou on 31 May. Both pilots had used up their ammunition, but were reluctant to break off the combat. Gubenko's ramming attack succeeded, for the IJNAF aircraft went down with a damaged wing. Gubenko, however, was able to bring his fighter home despite its damaged propeller. He received the Chinese Gold Order for his successful ramming attack. On 7 March 1939 he was awarded the title of Hero of the Soviet Union, but 24 days later Col Gubenko perished in a flying accident at Smolensk.

Gubenko's CO for much of his time in China was fellow ace Aleksey Blagoveshchenskiy, who fought with the CAF in the national liberation war from 5 December 1937 through to 10 August 1938. Initially serving as a squadron commander, he eventually became the volunteer fighter group commander. During this time Blagoveshchenskiy flew 117 sorties in both I-15bis and I-16s for a total of 125 operational flying hours. Engaging Japanese aircraft on 40 occasions, including twice at night, he scored seven personal and 16 shared victories. For these achievements Blagoveshchenskiy received the Combat Red Banner Order as well as a Chinese decoration. On 14 November 1938 Col Blagoveshchenskiy was awarded the title of Hero of the Soviet Union.

Later fighting in the Soviet-Finnish war as commander of 54th IAB, he completed a further 40+ combat sorties in the I-16 and participated in three air combats. During World War 2 Lt Gen Blagoveshchenskiy served in high command posts.

Another high-scoring ace who also saw combat in the Soviet-Finnish Winter War was Petr Kozachenko, who had arrived in China with the first group of volunteers in November 1937. Flying the I-16 over

Aleksey Blagoveshchenskiy fought with the CAF in the national liberation war from 5 December 1937 through to 10 August 1938. Initially serving as a squadron commander, he eventually became the volunteer fighter group commander. During this time Blagoveshchenskiy flew 117 combat sorties in both I-15bis and I-16s for a total of 125 operational flying hours. Engaging Japanese aircraft on 40 occasions, including twice at night, he scored seven personal and sixteen shared victories

Wuchang province, he shot down 11 enemy aircraft. Adding four more kills to his tally over Finland flying the I-153, Kozachenko was serving with 249th IAP when Germany invaded the USSR on 22 June 1941. The following day, flying an I-153, he shot down a Romanian He 112 as it crossed the border, and on 15 July added a German Bf 109 to his personal score. He scored further victories before the regiment was withdrawn for replenishment and conversion training in the autumn of 1941. Kozachenko subsequently flew LaGG-3, Yak-1 and La-5 fighters, and was awarded the title of Hero of the Soviet Union on 1 May 1943. He died in action near Danzig (Gdansk) on 18 March 1945 when he was serving as commander of 163rd GIAP, his combat record by then totalling 227 sorties and 27 personal and two shared victories.

Relations between the Soviet Union and Chiang Kai-shek's government had started to cool by late 1939, and in early 1940 Soviet military aid was cancelled and the volunteers withdrawn from China. Incomplete data for the period up to May of that year indicates that Soviet fighter pilots had fought in 50+ major air combats, shot down 81 aircraft and damaged another 114. They had also damaged 14 warships. Between 1938 and 1940, Soviet losses in China amounted to about 100 pilots killed in air combat and a similar number in accidents.

The last recorded victory scored by a Soviet volunteer pilot in China came on 10 January 1940, when 27 IJNAF bombers, escorted by 26 fighters, attacked Kweilin. A mixed formation of 14 I-15bis and seven I-16s attempted to attack the Japanese bombers, but five Polikarpovs were downed. Konstantin Kokkinaki, a brother of the famous record-breaking pilot Vladimir Kokkinaki, and a test pilot in his own right, claimed the only victory in return before his fighter was also hit. Spiralling out of the engagement, Kokkinaki had to use all of his skill as a pilot to prevent the fighter from crashing. This victory took Kokkinaki's final tally to seven kills in China.

He subsequently saw further action in the Great Patriotic War from June 1941 as commander of the 401st Special Purpose Fighter Air Regiment, which was staffed by experienced test pilots. Having scored three personal and four shared victories during World War 2, Kokkinaki continued his flying career as a test pilot post-war, being awarded the title of Hero of the Soviet Union on 21 August 1964.

CHINESE ACES

Chinese pilots flew both I-15bis and I-16s in combat against the Japanese from late 1937 through to mid-1941, achieving a significant number of kills in that time. Although this volume primarily details the exploits of Soviet aces, it should be noted that more than a dozen CAF pilots 'made ace' during the conflict with Japan, and at least half of these men made multiple

The I-153 made its combat debut in China with the CAF, this unmarked (and 'propellerless') example being one of around 100 supplied in 1939

claims with Polikarpov fighters. Indeed, China's leading ace, Liu Chi-Sheng, claimed the majority of his ten and two shared victories in Soviet-built aircraft.

Assigned to the 4th PG's 21st Pursuit Squadron (PS), he had scored his first two victories in August 1937 flying the Hawk III. Liu Chi-Sheng's squadron had re-equipped with I-16 Type 5s by the time he claimed his next successes (two A5Ms) on 18 February

This Chinese I-16 Type 5 has had its ShKAS 7.62 mm machine guns in the wings replaced with Vickers-made weapons. The aircraft was reportedly assigned to the CAF's leading ace, Liu Chi-Sheng, who claimed the majority of his ten and two shared victories while flying Soviet fighters

1938, and he would down two more IJNAF fighters with the aircraft before the year was out. The 21st PS switched to I-15bis in 1939, and Liu Chi-Sheng downed two bombers with the biplane fighter in May and July of that year.

With all Soviet volunteers having been pulled out of China by the spring of 1940, CAF pilots such a Liu Chi-Sheng struggled manfully to defend Chinese cities from the JAAF and IJNAF, which had begun to introduce improved combat aircraft into service by this time. 1940 would see Liu Chi-Sheng claim no fewer than four bombers destroyed, three of them falling between 6 and 12 June over Chungking.

Fellow ace Kao You-Hsin also flew with the 21st PS, although he only joined the unit in early 1940. Sharing in the destruction of a Japanese bomber on 26 May for his first victory, he flew the I-15bis for much of that year, before switching to the I-16 in 1941. Kao You-Hsin's most successful day came on 22 May 1941 when he destroyed two IJNAF G3M bombers directly overhead the CAF's Chung Chuan Chun airfield, north of Lanzhou. He survived the conflict with eight and one shared victories to his name.

Unlike Kao You-Hsin, Liu Chung-Wu was a frontline fighter pilot when the conflict with Japan escalated into open warfare in July 1937. Initially serving as a flight leader with the Hawk III-equipped 25th PS, he transferred to the 23rd PS in February 1938. This unit flew both the I-15bis and I-16, and he claimed three victories in both types in 1938. Liu Chung-Wu's best day came on 29 April 1938 in the legendary clash over Wuhan, when he was credited with two IJNAF aircraft destroyed while flying an I-15bis.

A handful of other CAF pilots claimed multiple kills with Polikarpov fighters during the war, which combined with previous victories in western types such as the Hawk III or Gladiator to give them ace status. Zhu Jia-Xun, for example, scored the first three of his five kills in an I-15bis with the 8th PS in March-April 1938, before making the switch to the Gladiator I-equipped 32nd PS in the summer of that year. Chow Ting-Fong possibly claimed as many as five I-16 victories in 1938 with the 25th PS, although available records state that his only confirmed kill came in a Hawk III with the 34th PS in August 1937. Mao Ying-Chu also used a Hawk III to claim his first victory, after which he scored three kills in the I-15bis and one in the I-16. He led the 4th PG in the Wuhan battle of 29 April 1938.

An unidentified CAF pilot poses with his I-16 Type 10 in early 1941. Soviet pilots had been pulled out of China 12 months earlier

KHALKHIN GOL

In mid-1939, Polikarpov fighters were extensively used in the Soviet-Japanese conflict that was centred around the Khalkhin Gol River in the Nomonhan area of the Soviet-Mongolian province of Doronod. The river formed the border between Soviet territory and Japanese-administered Manchuria. This short but hard-fought war would become known for the extensive use of air power by both sides in their attempts to win control of the skies.

Lasting just 129 days from 11 May to 15 September, the undeclared war involved 120,000 Soviet and 80,000 Japanese troops and more than 600 aircraft, with each side losing upwards of 200 of the latter.

When hostilities commenced in May, the Soviet air group in the region was the 57th Special Corps Air Force. It was comprised of 70th IAP, equipped with 24 I-16s and 14 I-15bis, and 150th SAP (*Smeshanniy Aviatsionniy Polk* – Composite Aviation Regiment) with 29 SB bombers and 15 Polikarpov R-5 multi-purpose biplanes. In military circles at this time service in Mongolia was synonymous with career failure, as that country was considered to be a 'backwater'. As a result, both the pilots and aircraft involved were regarded as sub-standard at best. It is hardly surprising, therefore, that the first encounters with the JAAF over the Khalkhin Gol River resulted in defeat for the Soviets.

On 21 May JAAF Ki-27 fighters shot down an R-5 liaison aircraft that had been sent aloft to support the 6th Mongolian Cavalry Division as it reconnoitred the disputed border area. The next day, at 1220 hrs, three I-16s and two I-15bis fighters were flying a border patrol over the river when they were attacked by five more Ki-27s. The I-16 flown by a pilot by the name of Lysenkov became separated from the group and was shot down. Two days later, 28 I-16s and 35 I-15bis of 22nd IAP, led by Maj Glazykin, arrived in Bain Tumen from the Trans-Baikal region. However, the unit's pilots had been inadequately trained, prompting

This photograph, taken by Boris Vdovenko, is dated 1939 and modestly captioned 'Soviet fighters ready to take-off in Mongolia'. Both I-15bis wear the standard camouflage scheme of the period, and tactical numbers adorn their rudders. The small red star on their fins is probably a squadron marking. The I-15bis struggled in aerial combat with the more modern Ki-27 monoplane fighter

23rd AB (*Aviatsionniy Brigada* – Air Brigade) CO Col Kutsevalov to report that 'aviators from 22nd IAP have been reluctant to fly for fear of crashing, when they should have been improving their flying proficiency and practising group combat skills'.

Nevertheless, on 25 May 22nd IAP was moved nearer to the frontier and re-deployed to Tamsag Bulag airfield. Following its arrival at the latter base, VVS RKKA strength in the area was boosted to 51 I-16s and 49 I-15bis. But the enemy had also increased its military presence in Manchuria when, on 24 May, an additional 20 Ki-27s of the JAAF had been flown in to Hailar – there were now 52 combat-ready fighters opposing Soviet forces. Two days later several of them encountered 18 I-16s over Lake Buir Nor. The Japanese pilots claimed to have shot down nine Polikarpovs, but Soviet sources deny that any sorties were flown that day, suggesting that this combat might have happened on the 27th.

On the latter date, three morning patrols by six I-16s of 22nd IAP (led by Sen Lt Cherenkov) failed to encounter the enemy. But when the regiment sortied for a fourth time, its fighters were intercepted by nine Ki-27s. Approaching the frontier in a loose formation, the I-16s met their Japanese counterparts at an altitude of 6500-7000 ft. A brief battle ensued, which ended in Cherenkov being shot down, Pyankov bailing out of his burning aircraft and Savchenko being killed while attempting a forced landing. The remaining three fighters escaped, but two of them had sustained serious damage.

On 28 May the Soviet Command ordered that ten I-16s and ten I-15bis be despatched on a patrol. There are varying reports as to what happened next, with one source suggesting that ten I-16s returned without encountering the enemy, while another states that the ten I-15s engaged 15 to 18 enemy aircraft. What is known for sure is that three I-15bis definitely took off at 0700 hrs and were attacked by a larger group of Ki-27s over the Khalkhin Gol River. All three Soviet machines were downed, killing their pilots, Voznesenskiy, Ivanchenko and Chekmarev.

At 1000 hrs ten more I-15bis from 22nd IAP were led away from Tamsag Bulag airfield by Capt Balashov. While patrolling overhead the Khalkhin Gol River crossings they were attacked by 18 Ki-27s, which immediately took advantage of their superior numbers in a swift battle. Six more Soviet pilots were killed, one bailed out of his stricken aircraft and another made a forced landing. Only Balashov and Gavrilov were able to bring their fighters home.

Although there remains some dispute as to the overall number of I-15bis that took part in the disastrous patrols of 28 May, what is clear is that I-16s did not participate in the battles that day. Two separate groups of three and ten I-15bis appear to have taken off, although JAAF pilots claimed to have shot down a total of 42 I-15bis and I-16s! Such exaggeration would become regular Japanese practice during the campaign. They did, however, admit losing one Ki-27 on 28 May, while the Soviets made no claims. One result of these defeats was a temporary ban on combat sorties following an order issued by K Voroshilov, Soviet Peoples' Commissar for Defence.

The poor showing by the Polikarpov biplane on the 28th had, to some extent, been anticipated by the VVS RKKA, which had ordered the withdrawal of the less effective 70th IAP to Bain Tumen airfield for

70th IAP squadron commander Maj Sergey Gritsevets (left) was one of a number of Spanish War aces rushed to Mongolia in late May 1939 to help bolster the Soviet fighter effort in-theatre. Having enjoyed great success over Spain, he increased his personal score by 12 victories during the Khalkhin Gol conflict. On 23 August Gritsevets performed the heroic act of landing his I-16 on the steppe amid enemy troops to rescue his CO, Maj V Zabaluev (right), who had been forced to bail out 60 kilometres behind Japanese lines

conversion to new aircraft and the replenishment of its pilots 48 hours before the decimation of 22nd IAP.

On 29 May a group of expert fighter pilots, some of them veterans of the Spanish Civil War, arrived in Mongolia under the command of Y Smushkevich, deputy head of the air force. Flying in from Moscow aboard three DC-3 transports, the group of 48 included Sergey Gritsevets, Nikolay Gerasimov, Aleksander Gusev, Stepan Danilov, Sergey Denisov, Nikolay Zherdev, Aleksander Zaytsev, Pavel Korobkov, Viktor Kustov, Ivan Lakeev, Viktor Matyunin, Boris Smirnov, Viktor Smirnov, Platon Smelyakov and Andrey and Evgeniy Stepanov. Most of these pilots would become aces in the coming conflict.

Heroes of the Khalkhin Gol conflict pose for a photograph near war's end. They are, from left to right, 70th IAP squadron commander Sergey Gritsevets, chief technical officer I Prachik, 22nd IAP CO Grigoriy Kravchenko, 70th IAP squadron commander P Korobkov, and 70th IAP Piloting Technique Inspector Boris Smirnov. Gritsevets, Kravchenko and Smirnov all achieved ace status in the campaign

There was a relative lull in the air fighting over Mongolia for almost a month, with little combat reported until 17 June. During this time the Soviet fighter force was significantly increased to the point where 70th IAP had 60 I-16 and 24 I-15bis fighters on strength by mid June, while 22nd IAP had 35 I-16s and 32 I-15bis. The VVS RKKA detachment in Mongolia was also re-designated the 1st Army Group Air Force during this period, and it established a group of 'airfields' (little more than steppeland cleared of scrub) around the border town of Tamsag Bulag.

The arrival of additional aircraft emboldened the VVS RKKA, which could now field 150 fighters compared to the JAAF's 78, to generate a number of raids on 22 June against Japanese ground positions along the Khalkhin Gol River. These resulted in a series of major air battles taking place that lasted for about two-and-a-half hours, with fresh groups of fighters succeeding others in what became three consecutive combats.

On the Soviet side, 105 aircraft (56 I-16s and 49 I-15bis of 22nd and 70th IAPs) were engaged, while VVS RKKA sources claim that the JAAF fielded up to 120 fighters. For their part, the Soviet pilots reported shooting down 25 Japanese aircraft for the loss of 17 of their own – 13 shot down and four destroyed on the ground. The casualties were mostly suffered by pilots flying the I-15bis, which had already been acknowledged as being less effective in combat against the Ki-27. The JAAF admitted the loss of seven aircraft, but claimed nearly 50 victories.

A graphic description of the events of 22 June was provided by one of the participants, future high-scoring ace Arseniy Vorozheykin. Experiencing his first air combat, he recalled;

'Having started up my engine, I saw fighters taking off from the adjacent airfield. We took off next. The squadron approached Khalkhin Gol in compact order. High above us we saw a flight of Japanese fighters. Squadron commander Capt Vasiliy Gugashin was determined to hunt down the enemy at any cost. He began chasing the Japanese at full throttle, leaving his wingmen far behind. The formation became stretched and scattered. The enemy flight, however, had the advantage of height and escaped. My CO abandoned the chase and swerved away.

'Meanwhile, far away to the left of us was a large swarm of aircraft. At first I thought they were our own fighters from the leading group, but there were too many of them – they numbered about 60 aircraft. And the way they flew was somewhat strange too. They were advancing with self-assurance and precision as if they felt themselves to be lords of the Mongolian sky. I tried to warn my commander by rocking my wings, but he wouldn't pay any attention! He was focused on another formation ahead of us that were almost certainly friendly aircraft. He hadn't seen the Japanese machines. So with a few other pilots I broke away from our commander's course to meet the actual enemies. At that point I didn't see anything but the enemy fighters ahead.

'All of a sudden something happened – an avalanche came down on the Japanese flight from somewhere above. Their strike was powerful and unexpected to the extent that it seemed as if a tremendous explosion had scattered the enemy formation, leaving burning aircraft behind. Then the "mad dance" began. Although initially overwhelmed by the sudden attack, I quickly spotted more JAAF fighters coming to the rescue of their friends. We had to intercept them, so we rushed to meet the newcomers face-to-face, attacking head-on. There would be no swerving away!

'I'd read a lot about head-on attacks, and had also heard stories of aces heroically rushing headlong at the enemy! How much skill, and will, would it take to win and survive such an attack? Everything inside me tensed up like a string as I held my breath. But the enemy fighters grew in size all too quickly. Instinctively, I pressed the machine gun buttons without aiming. Streams of fire shot in front of my fighter and suddenly the Japanese aircraft were gone. I just couldn't believe it was all over. I kept on flying in tense anticipation of the fatal crash – neither I or my enemy had turned away, or so I believed.

'And what had happened to the others? I recovered myself and looked around. The air was swarming with aircraft and streaming with fire. It looked to me as if the sky itself was on fire and a mad wind was blowing in to fan the flames, lashing and spinning everything around me. I was utterly lost and had no idea what to do. All my previous ideas about air combat had nothing to do with what was going on around me. You just couldn't tell friends from the Japanese. Everything was confused.'

It was indeed a large-scale melee, with friend mistaken for foe resulting in losses to friendly fire.

The Japanese struck back at the airfields surrounding Tamsag Bulag on 27 June, when 30 JAAF bombers escorted by 74 fighters hit them twice. 22nd IAP did its best to defend these sites, its pilots flying four or five sorties a day during late June and into early July. On 2 July two Japanese divisions crossed the Khalkhin Gol River into Mongolia, where they came under heavy attack from 60 SB-2 bombers, escorted by Polikarpov fighters. The resulting

Arseniy Vorozheykin studies a map in front of a Yak-7B in 1943 during World War 2. Four years earlier, while flying the I-16 with 22nd IAP in Mongolia, he had undertaken more than 160 combat sorties and fought in 30 aerial battles, during which he was credited with six individual and twelve shared victories. In World War 2 Vorozheykin flew 300+ combat sorties, participated in 90 aerial engagements and increased his tally to 52 personal and 13 shared victories

Pilots from 22nd IAP relax between sorties with a game of dominoes at an airfield near Tamsag Bulag in the summer of 1939. The I-16 Type 10 behind them bears the horizontal fin stripe unique to this regiment

22nd IAP commissar Vladimir Kalachev is seen here with an I-153 displaying the tactical number 11. In the Khalkhin Gol conflict, Kalachev shot down two Japanese fighters during the course of nine aerial engagements, and on 29 August 1939 he was awarded the title of Hero of the Soviet Union. Made CO of MiG-3-equipped 15th IAP in late 1941, Kalachev was shot down and killed on 28 June 1942 near Belgorod. He had by then increased his score to six individual and two shared aerial victories

Evgeniy Stepanov fought in Spain between 20 August 1937 and 27 July 1938, and as commander of an I-15 squadron he shot down eight to ten enemy aircraft (some at night). In Mongolia he displayed his ability as a fighter pilot to great effect. Serving with 22nd IAP, Stepanov commanded a squadron that was initially equipped with the I-15bis, but which later converted to the I-153 and I-16. During the conflict he flew more than 100 combat sorties, engaged in 40 aerial combats and shot down two JAAF aircraft, for which, on 29 August 1939, he was awarded the title of Hero of the Soviet Union. Stepanov also saw action in the Soviet-Finnish war with 19th IAP, and continued to hold command appointments in World War 2

dogfights with JAAF fighters often involved more than 100 aircraft, and the I-15bis units suffered some serious losses to the Ki-27s.

Having already flown seven sorties that day, pilots from 22nd IAP were ordered to escort an evening raid by SB-2s on 4 July. By then, however, combat fatigue had taken the edge off the Soviet pilots' performance, resulting in a number of losses. One of those to be shot down was Arseniy Vorozheykin, who had destroyed a Ki-27 the previous day. Hit dogfighting with a Japanese fighter, in the ensuing forced landing his aircraft nosed over. The badly wounded pilot was rescued by Mongolian border guards and flown to a hospital in Chita. There, the diagnosis was 'compression fracture of three lumbar vertebrae', which meant he was grounded. Vorozheykin subsequently 'lost' the documentation relating to his condition, however, and returned to his regiment in August.

During his time in Mongolia, Arseniy Vorozheykin flew more than 160 combat sorties, fought in 30 aerial combats and personally shot down six enemy aircraft and shared in the destruction of 12 more. For these achievements he was awarded the Order of Red Banner and nominated to become a Hero of the Soviet Union. In addition to his flying duties during the Khalkhin Gol conflict, Vorozheykin also held the post of commissar of the 5th squadron of 22nd IAP.

A few months later, Vorozheykin was sent to the disputed Soviet-Finnish border, but he failed to add to his victory tally during what became known as the Winter War for he was restricted to flying reconnaissance and ground attack missions. He would see much combat in World War 2, enjoying great success with the Yak-7B and Yak-9T after initially seeing action in the I-153 and I-16. Awarded his second title of Hero of the Soviet Union for scoring 45 individual combat victories in World War 2, Vorozheykin flew more than 300 combat sorties, participated in 90 aerial engagements and claimed a total of 52 personal and 13 shared victories between 1939 and 1945.

WEAKEST LINK

Although the I-16 pilots had enjoyed success over the Khalkhin Gol, the I-15bis was proving to be the weak link in the Soviet military aviation

chain. It was a weakness that the Ki-27 pilots attempted to exploit, preferring to engage them rather than the I-16s and the I-153s that had recently arrived. By August 1939 the I-15bis had been virtually withdrawn from daytime combat in-theatre and re-deployed to less demanding roles such as reconnaissance or night patrols.

Even so, some pilots managed to achieve notable combat success with the type, including Spanish War ace Evgeniy Stepanov. Although his official record showed that he had scored no personal victories in Spain, he actually claimed to have

USUs Khalkin Gol 1937

Your Ref:2115407500/002

DATE	CHARGES DUE		DATE	PAYMENTS/ *ADJUSTMENTS		BALANCE
04.04.11			04.04.11	B/F		0.00
04.04.11	DEBIT	79.23	04.04.11	HGBEN	53.29-	79.06CR
			08.04.11	CWOOD	105.00-	53.12CR
11.04.11	DEBIT	79.23	11.04.11	HGBEN	53.29-	27.18CR
18.04.11	DEBIT	79.23	18.04.11	HGBEN	53.29-	1.24CR
25.04.11	DEBIT	79.23	25.04.11	HGBEN	53.29-	
02.05.11	DEBIT	79.23	02.05.11	HGBEN	53.29-	
			06.05.11	CWOOD	105.00-	80.30CR
09.05.11	DEBIT	79.23	09.05.11	HGBEN	53.29-	54.36CR
16.05.11	DEBIT	79.23	16.05.11	HGBEN	53.29-	28.42CR
23.05.11	DEBIT	79.23	23.05.11	HGBEN	53.29-	2.48CR
30.05.11	DEBIT	79.23	30.05.11	HGBEN	53.29-	23.46
06.06.11	DEBIT	79.23	06.06.11	CWOOD	105.00-	
			06.06.11	HGBEN	53.29-	55.60CR
13.06.11	DEBIT	79.23	13.06.11	HGBEN	53.29-	29.66CR
20.06.11	DEBIT	79.23	20.06.11	HGBEN	53.29-	3.72CR
27.06.11	DEBIT	79.23	27.06.11	HGBEN	53.29-	22.22
04.07.11	DEBIT	79.23	04.07.11	HGBEN	53.29-	
			04.07.11	CWOOD	105.00-	56.84CR
11.07.11	DEBIT	79.23	11.07.11	HGBEN	53.29-	30.90CR
18.07.11	DEBIT	79.23	18.07.11	HGBEN	53.29-	4.96CR

shot down eight to ten aircraft during the conflict. Indeed, he went on the record stating that 'Personally, I brought down four CR.32s, two Me 109s, one Ju 86, one Do 17 and two SM.81s – all of them near Aragon and Teruella'.

In Mongolia he displayed his ability as a fighter pilot to great effect. Serving with 22nd IAP, he commanded a squadron that was initially equipped with the I-15bis, but which later converted to the I-153 and I-16. During the conflict

he flew 100+ combat sorties, engaged in 40 aerial combats and shot down two aircraft, for which, on 29 August 1939, he was awarded the title of Hero of the Soviet Union. Stepanov fought in the Soviet-Finnish war with 19th IAP and continued to hold command appointments.

In an effort to counteract the poor performance of the I-15bis, the VVS RKKA introduced 20 mm cannon-armed I-16 Type 17s in late July, and these helped redress the balance in favour of the Soviet units, who always enjoyed a numerical advantage. A high-scoring ace who made full use of the new cannon-armed I-16 was Ivan Krasnoyurchenko of 22nd IAP. Claiming five individual and sixteen shared victories, on 5 August he was leading a group of nine fighters when he downed a Ki-27. Many years later Krasnoyurchenko recalled;

'We managed to force one Japanese pilot away from the main formation. Six of us surrounded him and we signalled him to land – we were over friendly territory, of course. Refusing to comply, he just kept turning his aircraft so as to stop us from firing at him, trying all the while to escape towards Japanese-held territory. But Dmitriy Medvedev and Nikolay Arsenin wouldn't let him go, cutting off his escape route with bursts of machine gun fire. Then this "Samurai" zoomed up and immediately dived vertically towards the ground. We thought he was committing suicide, but not at all. He bailed out, and when he landed he started running for the frontier, which was very close.

'Immediately deciding that he had to be stopped at all cost, I landed my I-16 alongside him, jumped out of the cockpit and pursued the Japanese pilot. When I was within 100 ft of him he decided that he'd had enough. Drawing his pistol, he fired at me three times, but missed. After that he stopped and raised his hands. I'd heard about Japanese tricks, and I couldn't believe that a Samurai would just give up and yield to captivity. I approached him cautiously, step by step, with my pistol at the ready.

'When I was 30 ft from him he suddenly pulled out another gun from underneath his jacket – he had ostentatiously dropped the first – and fired twice. This time the bullets narrowly missed my head, whizzing by my ear. I aimed and fired. The Japanese wavered, as I had hit him in the shoulder. I fired again and he collapsed. Soon afterwards, Mongolian horsemen arrived and I handed my wounded captive over to them.'

During the conflict in Mongolia, Lt Krasnoyurchenko served as a deputy squadron commander with 22nd IAP, flying 111 combat sorties,

The I-153 *Chayka* made its combat debut with the VVS RKKA in the Khalkhin Gol conflict, the aircraft proving capable of holding its own in aerial combat with the JAAF's Ki-27. It quickly replaced the I-15bis in-theatre, the latter having been targeted by the Japanese as the 'weak link' in the Soviet fighter arsenal

Lt Ivan Krasnoyurchenko of 22nd IAP completed 111 sorties over Mongolia in 1939, engaging JAAF aircraft 33 times and claiming five victories. He also attacked ground targets on 45 occasions. According to his comrades' recollections, Krasnoyurchenko's I-16 displayed a zigzag lightning bolt on the side of its fuselage

engaging in 33 aerial combats and shooting down five Japanese fighters. On 17 November he was awarded the title of Hero of the Soviet Union. In the summer of 1941 he was still serving with 22nd IAP, which had by then been re-deployed to Kiev. He shot down a German bomber on his first day in action.

Later, Krasnoyurchenko served with 43rd IAP and was promoted to command 92nd IAP and then 102nd and 147th IADs (*Istrebitelniy Aviatsionniy Diviziya* – Fighter Aviation Divisions) of the Air Defence Forces. He went on to score three more personal and 16 shared victories. By war's end Col Krasnoyurchenko had been appointed commander of 9th IAK (*Istrebitelniy Aviatsionniy Korpus* – Fighter Aviation Corps) of the Air Defence Forces.

ACES HIGH

The arrival of combat-experienced fighter pilots in Mongolia in late May certainly had a positive effect on the VVS RKKA's ability to take the fight to the clearly superior Ki-27-equipped JAAF units. By August Japanese losses in the air inspired a large-scale Soviet attack by 100,000 troops and 800 tanks across the Khalkhin Gol River into Manchuria. Supporting this offensive were more than 500 aircraft, with Soviet fighters targeting forward airfields in strafing attacks that saw the JAAF suffer still more losses to its precious Ki-27 fleet.

It was during this period that the high-scoring I-15bis and I-16 pilots really came to the fore, one such pilot being Spanish War veteran Maj Stepan Danilov, CO of 56th IAP during the Mongolian campaign. Flying 60 combat sorties, he shot down six enemy fighters and two bombers between July and September, which earned him the title of Hero of the Soviet Union on 17 November 1939.

Former test pilot Viktor Rakhov of 22nd IAP was another to enjoy success during this period of near continual combat. Having served in various fighter units and at the Air Force Research Institute for several years prior to being posted to the Khalkhin Gol area in May 1939, he was an expert on the I-16. Indeed, Snr Lt Rakhov had been a member of an aerobatic team in Moscow which performed regularly over Red Square and Tushino airfield.

Upon being transferred to Mongolia with the Smushkevich group, he was made a flight commander in 22nd IAP. Rakhov's service record in-theatre totalled 68 combat sorties, during which time he claimed eight personal and six shared victories. During his first sortie on 12 June he shot down a Ki-27, followed by a second example 48 hours later. Rakhov was himself forced to bail out moments later, however, and it took him two days to make it back to his base on foot. On 20 August Rakhov carried out a successful ramming attack on

22nd IAP pilots discuss a recent combat at an airfield near Tamsag Bulag. The I-16 Type 10 in the background, adorned with a red fin tip and white fin strip, was probably the aircraft flown by Snr Lt Viktor Rakhov (second from right), who scored eight victories during the Khalkhin Gol campaign

a Ki-27, but he managed to nurse his fighter back home. In his last air combat exactly one week later, Rakhov scored two further victories, but when flying back over the frontline towards Soviet territory his fighter was hit by flak and he received a serious stomach wound. Viktor Rakhov died in a hospital in Chita on 29 August. That same day he was posthumously awarded the title of Hero of the Soviet Union.

Another high-scoring ace to emerge in the summer of 1939 was Nikolay Zherdev, who had also made his combat debut in Spain the previous year. Flying both I-15s and I-16s with the Republicans from March to September 1938, he claimed three kills – all CR.32s. One of these came on 12 August when Zherdev destroyed a Fiat fighter by ramming it, having exhausted all of his ammunition. This was possibly the first example of a *Taran* attack, which subsequently became popular during the dark days of 1941-42 on the Eastern Front. On his return to the Soviet Union, he was awarded the Order of Lenin.

From 29 May to 16 September 1939, Zherdev commanded a squadron within 70th IAP in Mongolia. During this time he flew 105 combat sorties, participated in 46 aerial engagements and shot down 11 enemy aircraft, with three further victories shared. On 17 November Zherdev was awarded the title of Hero of the Soviet Union. Enjoying further success in World War 2, he was serving as navigation officer of 821st IAP when he was killed on 15 November 1942, together with his regimental commander, Maj M Sokolov. The pair were heading for a commanders' conference when their UTI-4 trainer crashed near the north Caucasian village of Batayurt. Zherdev's final tally in three wars was 16 personal and six shared victories.

Like Zherdev, Snr Lt Mitrofan Noga was also a squadron commander in 70th IAP. Engaged in the Khalkin Gol operation between 11 May and 16 September 1939, he flew 109 combat sorties, engaged in 22 aerial combats and shot down nine fighters and shared in the destruction of two bombers. Noga subsequently took part in the occupation of eastern Poland, and he was still here when, on 17 November, he was awarded the title of Hero of the Soviet Union. Promoted to command 41st IAP, Noga subsequently saw combat in the Great Patriotic War as CO of 182nd IAP of the Air Defence Forces, and later with 144th, 322nd and 256th IADs. Between 1939 and 1945 he flew 550 combat sorties, engaged in 120 aerial combats and scored 27 personal and three shared victories.

Fellow 70th IAP ace Aleksander Zaytsev arrived in Mongolia to assume command of the regiment having already claimed eight victories in Spain between 3 January and 14 August 1937. With combat experience in both the I-15bis and I-16, Zaytsev led 70th IAP from 11 May to 16 September 1939. He flew 29 combat sorties and shot down six enemy aircraft during this time, being awarded the title of Hero of the Soviet Union on 17 November 1939 for his exploits in both conflicts.

This I-16 Type 10 of 22nd IAP force-landed in Mongolia in the summer of 1939. An attrition replacement sent to Mongolia at the height of the conflict over the Khalkhin Gol River, this I-16 has had its fuselage identification markings painted out and a non-standard silver stripe applied around the rear fuselage. The latter was seen on a number of aircraft flown by 22nd IAP in July 1939, it being assumed that the stripe was applied to enable other Soviet aircraft to quickly identify I-16s from the regiment in the heat of battle

Ace Aleksander Zaytsev claimed victories in three wars, initially seeing combat in Spain between 3 January and 14 August 1937. Flying both the I-15 and I-16, he scored eight aerial victories. During the Khalkhin Gol conflict of 1939, Zaytsev commanded 70th IAP and shot down six more aircraft. He added a solitary kill to his tally in World War 2

Ranking Soviet China War ace Grigoriy Kravchenko (front) and technical officer of the 1st Army Group Ivan Prachik (passenger) relax by riding a motorcycle in Mongolia shortly after their arrival in-theatre. The hastily camouflaged DC-3 that had delivered them to Bain Tumen airfield on 2 June 1939 still displays the Douglas company logo beneath its cockpit. Kravchenko would claim a handful of victories over Mongolia whilst leading 22nd IAP and then see further action over Finland in the Winter War. During World War 2 he fought on the Bryansk, Kalinin, Leningrad and Volkhov fronts until he was killed in action on 23 February 1943 whilst serving as CO of 215th IAD

22nd IAP's Grigoriy Kravchenko was one of a handful of pilots sent to Mongolia who had seen previous combat in China in 1938. Having joined the VVS RKKA in 1933, a year later he was transferred to 116th OIAE near Moscow to participate in service testing of new fighters and armament. In February 1938, having been promoted to a senior lieutenant, Kravchenko was transferred to China, where he flew combat missions in both I-15bis and I-16s. By August his record showed that he had completed 76 combat sorties and fought in eight aerial engagements, shooting down three bombers and a fighter. On 22 February 1939 Maj Kravchenko was honoured with the title of Hero of the Soviet Union. In June he arrived in Mongolia, initially as an adviser to 22nd IAP and then as regimental commander following the death of Maj Glazykin.

On the 27th of that month Kravchenko pursued a Japanese Ki-15 reconnaissance aircraft and eventually shot it down over Manchuria, but the long pursuit deep into enemy territory resulted in his I-16 running out of fuel. Fortunately for him, he was able to make it across the Khalkhin Gol River and land in friendly territory. Nevertheless, it still took Kravchenko three days to make it back to base.

During his time in Mongolia Kravchenko engaged in eight aerial combats and achieved three personal and four shared victories. On 29 August he was awarded the title of Hero of the Soviet Union for a second time in the wake of his exemplary combat performance and heroism.

During the Soviet-Finnish war, Col Kravchenko commanded the Special Purpose Air Group, but details of his involvement in the unit's operations in the conflict remain elusive. He was appointed commander of the 11th Combined Air Division on the Western Front on 22 June 1941, and on 23 July 1942 Kravchenko was given command of 215th IAD. He continued to fly combat missions, and his comrades' memoirs say that his personal fighter was painted all-red during that period. Promoted to the rank of lieutenant general, Kravchenko was killed on 23 February 1943 when his La-5 was shot down in combat near Sinyavino, in the Leningrad region. Attempting to bail out from an altitude of just 1000 ft, his parachute had insufficient time to deploy before the veteran ace hit the ground. According to some reports, Kravchenko had shot down four enemy aircraft in his last battle – these would have been his only kills in World War 2.

Vitt Skobarikhin was one of Kravchenko's squadron commanders within 22nd IAP, seeing action in the Khalkhin Gol campaign from 27 May 1939. His service record shows that he flew 169 combat sorties and fought in 26 aerial battles, during which he shot down five aircraft and shared in the destruction of six more – one of his victories was

achieved in a ramming attack. On 29 August Snr Lt Skobarikhin was awarded the title of Hero of the Soviet Union.

ROCKET FIGHTER

One of the new weapons trialled by the VVS RKKA in this conflict was the RS-82 rocket, which was initially fitted to the I-16 from early August. The emergence of the 82 mm unguided rocket projectile as an aerial weapon for the Soviet fighter force had been preceded by a lengthy development and refinement process throughout the 1930s involving both the RS-82 rocket itself and the RO-82 launcher. The experimental installation of launchers on fighters had begun in 1934, and by mid-1939 the RS-82 was reliable enough to make its combat debut over Mongolia.

A group of I-16s equipped with eight RS-82 rockets under their wings duly flew 59 combat sorties between 8 August and 15 September 1939, participating in 16 aerial combats in which the rockets were fired, while on six missions the fighters' machine guns were used too.

According to the records from 22nd IAP, a group of I-16 fighters armed with RS-82 rockets and commanded by Capt N Zvonarev shot down 14 enemy fighters and three bombers during the weapon's trial period. This first operational deployment proved the effectiveness of the rocket projectiles as an air-to-air weapon against enemy aircraft (fighters or bombers), as well as its potency against infantry, cavalry, vehicle convoys and anti-aircraft and field artillery. More combat accounts detailing the RS-82's effectiveness appear in the final chapter.

TREATY

On 11 September 1939, with Soviet forces poised to destroy two Japanese divisions on the eastern side of the Khalkhin Gol River, the first heavy snow of the winter came, effectively grounding the VVS RKKA and halting the advance of the Red Army. Sporadic air combat continued for a further five days until the undeclared war was ended with the signing of a treaty by both sides.

By then the VVS RKKA had claimed 589 victories for the loss of 207 aircraft (160 of which were fighters) and 211 men killed. Actual documented losses according to the JAAF totalled 162 aircraft. The claims made by Japanese fighter pilots were even more fanciful, as they were credited with destroying a whopping 1162 Soviet aircraft in the air and 98 on the ground!

More than a dozen Soviet pilots had 'made ace' in the conflict, and these men returned to units in western USSR that already boasted aviators who had seen action in Spain and/or China. Having seen off the challenge of the JAAF, the VVS RKKA's Polikarpov units now prepared themselves for combat with an enemy that was far closer to Moscow – Finland.

Vitt Skobarikhin was a squadron commander with 22nd IAP, seeing action in the Khalkhin Gol campaign from 27 May 1939. His service record shows that he flew 169 combat sorties and fought in 26 aerial battles, during which he shot down five aircraft and shared in the destruction of six more – one of his victories was achieved in a ramming attack

Skobarikhin's I-16 Type 10 survived his 20 July 1939 ramming attack on a Ki-27, despite the fighter having suffered severe damage to its left wing. Note the red star, outlined in white, on the propeller spinner

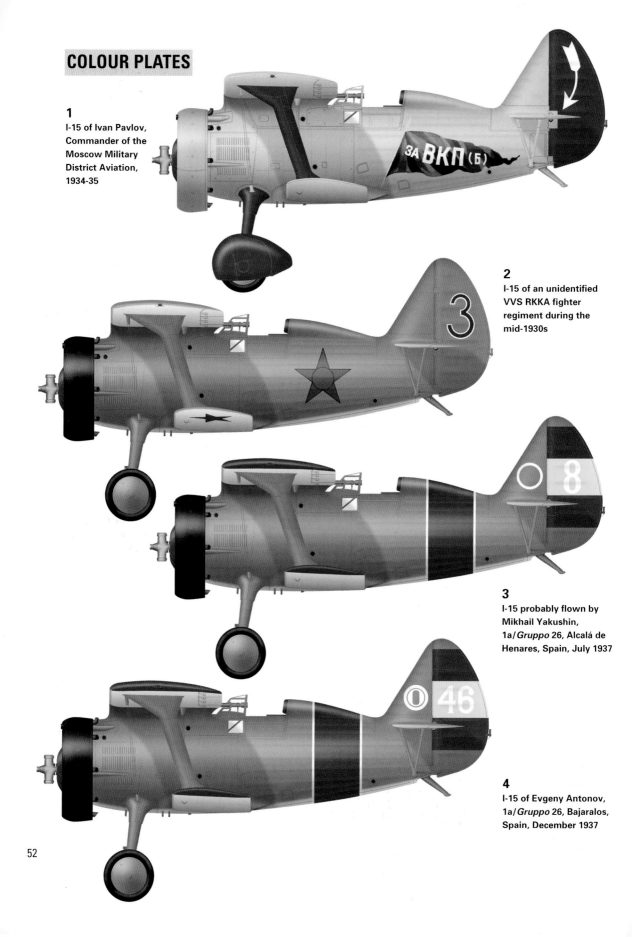

COLOUR PLATES

1
I-15 of Ivan Pavlov,
Commander of the
Moscow Military
District Aviation,
1934-35

2
I-15 of an unidentified
VVS RKKA fighter
regiment during the
mid-1930s

3
I-15 probably flown by
Mikhail Yakushin,
1a/*Gruppo* 26, Alcalá de
Henares, Spain, July 1937

4
I-15 of Evgeny Antonov,
1a/*Gruppo* 26, Bajaralos,
Spain, December 1937

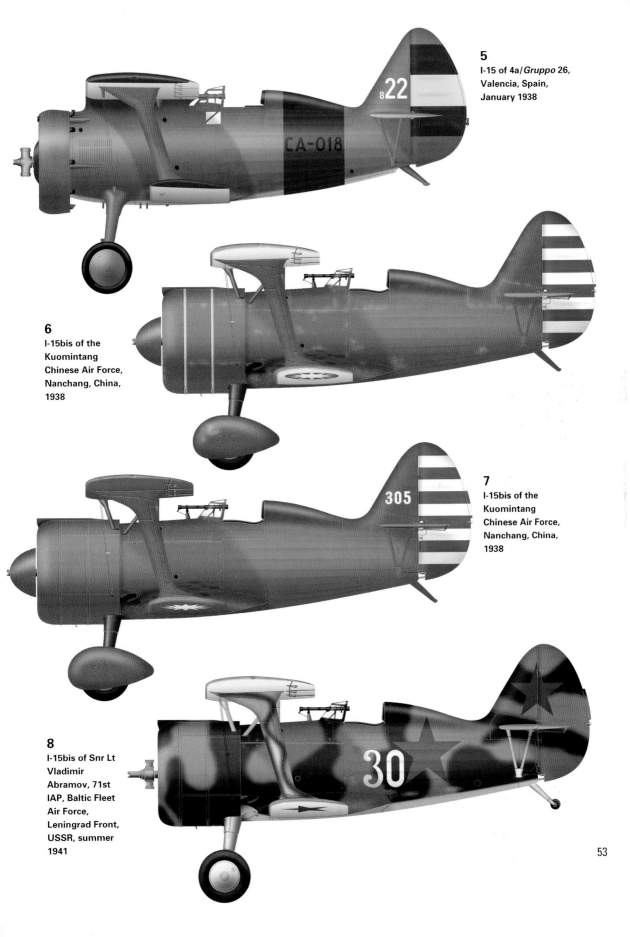

5
I-15 of 4a/*Gruppo* 26,
Valencia, Spain,
January 1938

6
I-15bis of the
Kuomintang
Chinese Air Force,
Nanchang, China,
1938

7
I-15bis of the
Kuomintang
Chinese Air Force,
Nanchang, China,
1938

8
I-15bis of Snr Lt
Vladimir
Abramov, 71st
IAP, Baltic Fleet
Air Force,
Leningrad Front,
USSR, summer
1941

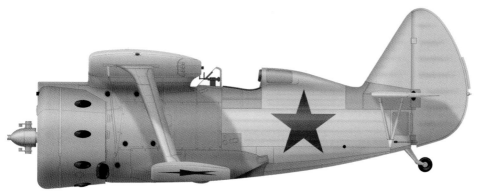

9
I-153 of 22nd IAP, 1st Army Group Air Force, Tamsag Bulag, Mongolia, early summer 1939

10
I-153 of Vladimir Kalachev, 22nd IAP, 1st Army Group Air Force, Tamsag Bulag, Mongolia, August 1939

11
I-153 of Lt Sergey Zhukovskiy, 127th IAP, Western Military District, Leningrad Front, USSR, summer 1941

12
I-153 of Snr Lt Aleksander Adonkin, 72nd SAP, Northern Fleet Air Force, Vaenga, USSR, summer 1941

13
I-153 of Snr Lt
Aleksander Baturin,
71st IAP, Baltic
Fleet Air Force,
Bychye Pole, USSR,
summer 1942

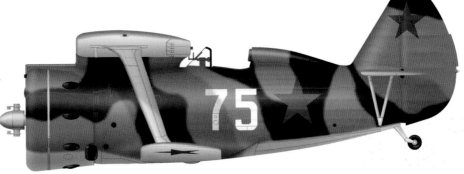

14
I-153 of Capt Petr
Biskup, 71st IAP,
Baltic Fleet Air Force,
Bychye Pole, USSR,
summer 1942

15
I-16 Type 5 of
5 *Escuadrilla/Grupo
de Caza*, Spain, late
1937

16
I-16 Type 5 of
5 *Escuadrilla/Grupo
de Caza*, Spain,
summer 1937

17
I-16 Type 5 of
5 *Escuadrilla/Grupo
de Caza*, Cartagena,
Spain, summer 1937

18
I-16 Type 10 of
Grigoriy Kravchenko,
Kuomintang Chinese
Air Force, Hankou,
China, April 1938

19
I-16 Type 10 of the
Kuomintang Chinese
Air Force, Hankou,
China, summer 1938

20
I-16 Type 10 of 70th IAP,
1st Combat Air Group,
Tamsag Bulag, Mongolia,
May 1939

21

I-16 Type 10 of Snr Lt Viktor Rakhov, 22nd IAP, 1st Combat Air Group, Tamsag Bulag, Mongolia, summer 1939

22

I-16 Type 10 of 22nd IAP, 1st Combat Air Group, Tamsag Bulag, Mongolia, July-August 1939

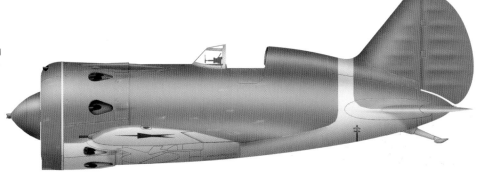

23

I-16 Type 10 of Snr Lt Vitt Skobarikhin, 22nd IAP, 1st Combat Air Group, Tamsag Bulag, Mongolia, summer 1939

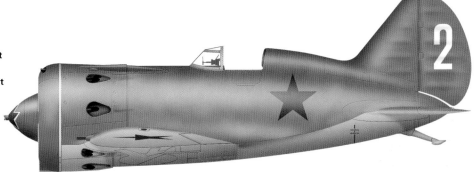

24

I-16 Type 10 of Snr Lt Leonid Galchenko, 145th IAP, Vaenga, USSR, summer 1941

25
I-16 Type 10 of Snr Lt
Nikolay Ignatyev,
728th IAP, Kalinin
Front, USSR, winter
1942-43

26
I-16 Type 10 of Maj Gen
Ivan Lakeev, 235th IAD,
Kuban Front, USSR, late
1941

27
I-16 Type 17 of Snr Lt
Arseniy Vorozheykin,
22nd IAP, 1st Combat
Air Group, Tamsag
Bulag, Mongolia,
August 1939

28
I-16 Type 17 of Snr Lt
Mikhail Vasilyev, 4th GIAP,
Baltic Fleet Air Force,
Novaya Ladoga, USSR,
spring 1942

29
I-16 Type 24 of Snr Lt
Nikolay Terekhin,
161st IAP,
Belorussian Front,
USSR, summer 1941

30A (left)
I-16 Type 24 of Snr Lt
Vasiliy Golubev, 7th
IAP, Leningrad Front,
USSR, summer 1941

30B (right)
I-16 Type 24 of Snr Lt
Vasiliy Golubev, 7th
IAP, Leningrad Front,
USSR, summer 1941

31
I-16 Type 24 of Snr Lt
Anatoliy Lomakin,
21st IAP, Baltic Sea
Air Force, Leningrad
Front, USSR, 1942-43

32
I-16 Type 24 of Snr Lt
Gennadiy Tsokolaev,
4th GIAP, Baltic Fleet
Air Force, Leningrad
Front, USSR,
February 1942

33
I-16 Type 24 of Lt
Krichevskiy, 254th IAP,
Budogoshch, near
Leningrad, USSR, 1943

34
I-16 Type 24 of Sgt
Grigoriy Guryanov, 4th
GIAP, Baltic Fleet Air
Force, Leningrad Front,
USSR, spring 1942

35
I-16 Type 24 of 13th
OIAE, Baltic Fleet Air
Force, Nizino, USSR,
summer 1940

36A (left)
I-16 Type 24 of Snr Lt
Boris Safonov, 72nd
SAP, Northern Fleet
Air Force, Vaenga,
USSR, summer 1941

36B (right)
I-16 Type 24 of Snr Lt
Boris Safonov, 72nd
SAP, Northern Fleet
Air Force, Vaenga,
USSR, summer 1941

37
I-16 Type 24 of Snr
Sgt S Surjenko, 72nd
SAP, Northern Fleet
Air Force, Vaenga,
USSR, summer 1941

38
I-16 Type 29 of Snr Lt
Petr Brinko, 13th IAP,
Baltic Fleet Air Force,
Leningrad Front,
USSR, summer 1941

WINTER WAR

War broke out between the Soviet Union and Finland on 30 November 1939 and continued until 13 March 1940. The root cause of this conflict was the USSR's failure to bully Finland into giving it use of the latter country's land and bases in order to safeguard the approaches to Leningrad through the Gulf of Finland should Germany decide to attack. Most of the action took place along the frontier area between Vaida Guba, the northern part of the Rybachiy Peninsula and Kurort railway station to the west of Sestroretsk. This battleground covered 950 miles of territory, and included part of the huge Lake Ladoga and the vital Karelian Isthmus in the south.

Well aware of Soviet plans, the Finns had constructed a formidable series of defensive positions known as the Mannerheim Line across the Karelian Isthmus, as this neck of land was the direct line of approach for an invading army heading for the town of Viipuri and then onto to the Finnish capital, Helsinki. Supporting the troops on the ground, the Finnish Air Force numbered just 145 aircraft, of which 114 were serviceable when war broke out. Its primary fighter was the Fokker D.XXI, which equipped two squadrons, although one flight was still flying obsolete Bristol Bulldog biplanes.

The VVS RKKA, by comparison, had a large force of fighters and bombers at its disposal. Indeed, the fighter regiments involved in the campaign operated three types of aircraft, namely the I-15bis, I-16 and I-153. The following table shows fighter distribution by type across the various frontline sectors at different stages in the war;

	30/11/39	1/1/40	1/2/40	6/3/40
Northwest Front*	665	701	709	760
15th Army Air Force**	-	-	-	138
8th Army Air Force	75	80	109	131
9th Army Air Force	15	93	138	140
14th Army Air Force	50	74	86	85
Special Air Group***	-	33	68	126
Total	**805**	**981**	**1110**	**1380**
Aircraft type				
I-16	410	474	453	427
I-153	119	194	354	578
I-15	276	313	303	365

*Including the Northwestern Front Air Force, Leningrad Air Defence Forces and 7th and 13th Army Air Forces
**15th Army Air Force was formed on 18 February 1940
***Special Air Group Air Force entered combat on 21 December 1939

As the war developed, the strength of the various Soviet air forces/ groups in the frontline was steadily increased thanks to the arrival of additional bombers and I-153s. The I-16 ranks built up far slower, reaching a total deployed strength of 474 aircraft in January. By the end of the war, however, this figure had dropped to 427 examples of all versions remaining in a combat-ready state in the frontline. The I-15bis represented about 30 per cent (276 aircraft) of the Soviet fighters committed, with 88 more operated by 61st and 10th ABs of the Baltic Fleet Air Force.

At the start of the conflict the distribution of I-153s in Red Army units was as follows – 102 fighters operated by the 7th Army Air Force (including 47 detached to the Leningrad Military District Air Force) and a squadron of 17 fighters in 56th SAP attached to the 14th Army. In the Baltic Fleet Air Force, only 22 of its 246 fighters were I-153s, and these were operated by 61st and 10th ABs.

After air attacks against Finnish forces by bomber units based in Estonia on the first two days of the war, poor weather then blighted the area for the next three weeks. Such conditions had not affected Snr Lt Fedor Shinkarenko on 1 December, however, when he became the first Soviet fighter pilot to shoot down an enemy aircraft in the conflict. A squadron commander with 7th IAP, 59th IAB, he had led five I-16 elements of the 4th Squadron in an interception of Finnish aircraft in the Lake Kaukjarve area. Having spotted the enemy, Shinkarenko led his squadron over the Kurelja road and quickly singled out a 'fighter-type aircraft' flying over Lake Juskjarvi at an altitude of about 5000 ft. Shinkarenko subsequently reported;

'Our I-16s, flown by Senior Political Officer G Didenko, Lt Grigoryev and myself, opened fire on the aircraft, which attempted to avoid combat. It went into a 60- to 70-degree dive. Two attempts to level out failed, and after the second it continued diving to an altitude of 300-250 ft, at which point we lost sight of it in the smoke that rose up to about that height and completely blocked our view. All the pilots believe the aircraft much have hit the ground.'

They had attacked a Bulldog, and its pilot, Flt Sgt T Uuttu, survived the ensuing crash-landing, although his aircraft was destroyed. Uuttu also claimed that he had shot down one of his attackers with a short burst of fire prior to his demise. For his achievements, and claiming two other kills during the course of 46 sorties that saw him escorting

His fighter already ticking over behind him, an I-15bis pilot receives last minute instructions prior to flying a hazardous low-level tactical reconnaissance mission during the Winter War

Snr Lt Fedor Shinkarenko of 7th IAP poses with his I-16 Type 10 during the Soviet-Finnish war. He flew 46 combat sorties and shot down three enemy aircraft during the latter conflict, and on 7 April 1940 he was awarded the title of Hero of the Soviet Union. During the Great Patriotic War Shinkarenko flew several dozen combat sorties in various versions of the Yak fighter, adding a further five kills to his trio of Winter War victories

Pilots of 7th IAP conduct a preflight briefing for the benefit of the camera. Fedor Shinkarenko is standing fourth from left, while second from left, looking directly at him, is future ace Petr Pokryshev. Claiming his first victory in the Finnish campaign, Pokryshev would score ten individual and seven shared victories with the I-16 during the Great Patriotic War. He survived the conflict with 38 individual and eight shared victories to his name, his aerial feats twice earning the title of Hero of the Soviet Union

This I-15bis of 13th OIAE was flown by the Hero of the Soviet Union Battalion Commissar Volosevich, the fighter bearing the inscription *For Stalin!* over its red star

bombers and attacking enemy airfields and troops, Shinkarenko received the title of Hero of the Soviet Union on 7 April 1940.

In July 1941, having attained the rank of a major, he was appointed commander of 42nd IAP, which was renamed 133rd GIAP in February 1944. In July of that year there was further promotion, this time to commander of 130th IAD. During World War 2 Shinkarenko flew several dozen combat sorties in various versions of the Yak fighter, and he added a further five kills to his trio of Winter War victories.

His aerial success on 1 December 1939 was a rare one for the VVS RKKA fighter force, as reduced visibility caused pilots to lose their bearings in the air. This meant that most Polikarpov units stayed on the ground, adversely affecting the number of bomber escort missions flown. By the middle of the month, as conditions improved, the ice on the various lakes in the area was up to 20 cm thick – enough to support the operation of fighters. In the Leningrad area frozen lakes had been prepared to operate aircraft by mid-January 1940.

With clearing skies, most fighter units spent the bulk of their time attacking ground targets. Indeed, in the Air Forces of the 8th, 9th and 14th Armies, such missions accounted for up to 90 per cent of the total combat sorties flown. As the initial priority for the air forces was the destruction of communications links in Finland, most strikes were flown against rail infrastructure.

Few large-scale aerial actions took place during the first two months of the campaign, although when opposing forces clashed it was the Finnish D.XXI units that usually emerged victorious – some 50 Soviet aircraft had been credited to both squadrons by the end of 1939. This was particularly true when the Finns counterattacked in the Karelian Isthmus to the north of Lake Ladoga on 6 January, the Fokkers downing eight DB-3 bombers.

In response to Finnish gains on the ground, the VVS RKKA stepped up its aerial attacks to cover a big build-up of troops. Despite increased fighter cover, Soviet bomber units suffered more heavy losses between 17 and 20 January, with 27 aircraft being downed.

With the Polikarpov units now wary of engaging the D.XXIs, they switched their attention to the Finnish bomber force instead. This proved to be a successful tactic, as a handful of Blenheim I/IVs were destroyed in late January.

This ski-equipped I-16 Type 5 was assigned to 13th OIAE, 61st IAB of the Baltic Fleet Air Force, and on 4 February 1940 Snr Lt Boruzdin returned to base with the fighter's rudder badly damaged after it had been hit by anti-aircraft fire over Lake Bjerke

In the first week of February the Red Army launched a massive and ultimately successful offensive towards Viipuri. Finnish units, now bolstered by the arrival of Gloster Gladiators and Fiat G.50s, attempted to repulse the large Soviet bomber formations that sortied in support of the offensive, but improved tactics by the Polikarpov units resulted in the aerial engagements being less one-sided in favour of the Finns.

From a VVS RKKA perspective, most of the Winter War activity involved elements of the Northwestern Front Air Force. The latter reported six major air combats and 65 minor engagements during the campaign, and some of the more significant actions that took place in support of the push on Viipuri were detailed in a document created by the air force post-war entitled *Combat Performance of the Red Army Air Force in the War with Finland*;

'On 2 February the fighters of 59th AB of the 7th Army Air Force found themselves caught up in an air battle. A flight commander who had just returned from a reconnaissance mission reported sighting enemy aircraft near a lake north of Vuoksenniska railway station. Fifteen fighters took off immediately, led by deputy regimental commander Capt Bushev. The attack group comprised three I-16s and three I-153s, escorted by nine more I-16s.

'Near Imatra railway station the entire group encountered heavy flak. The aircraft took evasive action but the strike force and its escort became separated. The Finnish fighters had by then already taken off, and nine I-16s of the escort were attacked from the down-sun direction by up to 20 D.XXIs. The battle began at an altitude of about 1250 ft, and the timely arrival of the six-fighter strike force resulted in two enemy fighters being shot down. The combatants paired off, and by the end of the battle a total of 12 Finnish fighters were reported to have been shot down without loss to the Soviet fighters. The Finns, however, admitted losing only one D.XXI.

'On 25 February two flights from 149th IAP were attacked by eight D.XXIs as they strafed a train. The I-16 pilots reported scoring four victories without loss. Later in the day, two flights of I-16s from 68th IAP of the 13th Army Air Force were escorting nine SB bombers when they were engaged by nine Bristol Bulldog fighters near Melkela. The I-16 pilots emerged from the 12-minute combat to report scoring five victories without loss, although three of the Soviet fighters received about 40 bullet holes.

'The next day fighters of 149th IAP escorted SBs targeting Kouvala railway station, and they shot down three D.XXIs from a force of 12, as well as a monoplane of undetermined type. On 29 February I-16s of 68th IAP, 15th AB, flew a reconnaissance mission along the River Vuoksa. Finnish Gladiator fighters took off from a frozen lake near Vuoksenniska railway station to intercept the raiders. One was destroyed attempting to take-off and another was shot down while climbing. After that the I-16s withdrew, only to make a follow-up attack on the makeshift Finnish airfield a short while later.

'The 23 aircraft led by Maj Gil comprised nine I-16s and three I-153s, escorted by eight I-16s and three I-153s. This time, however, the Finnish fighters were on the alert, and they quickly took off from their frozen lake base when Soviet fighters were detected seven miles away. Several more

Pilots from 13th OIAE pose in front of an I-16 Type 17 during the Winter War

Capt Petr Petrov is seen in the cockpit of his I-15bis. A future ace, he would make a handful of claims in the aircraft while serving as a squadron commander with 68th IAP, 13th Army Air Force of the Northwestern Front in the Winter War. During a combat mission on 17 February 1940 he landed his biplane fighter on the frozen surface of Lake Muola-Jarvi under enemy fire in order to rescue a comrade who had made a forced landing. For this exploit Petrov was awarded the title of Hero of the Soviet Union on 7 April 1940

took off from another airfield near the target.

'Snr Lt Efimov, leading the escort fighters, attacked an aircraft from the second group of Finnish machines, and the official report of the action stated that his I-16 entered a steep dive and crashed. After the initial attack, the combat continued as a series of battles between individual aircraft and two-fighter elements. The enemy force was estimated at 27 Fokker D.XXIs and Gladiators. On their return the Soviet pilots reported shooting down 18 of them.

In addition to Efimov, Lt Volokhov was also lost, but in neither case was the type of enemy aircraft involved reported. The Finns later admitted losing five Gladiators of the 26th Squadron and one D.XXI of the 24th Squadron that day.

'On 2 March 17 I-153s on a bomber escort mission engaged 15 D.XXIs in the Tampere area. Two Fokkers were reportedly shot down, but the number of Soviet losses was not disclosed. That same day nine I-153s attacked 11 D.XXIs also near Tampere, but the Finns avoided combat. The Finnish side reported losing one Bulldog on 2 March.

'Soviet and Finnish fighters were again in combat a week later, on the 9th, over the northern part of Kojvisto Peninsula. Five I-153s of 59th IAB of the 7th Army Air Force encountered what were reported to have been eight Finnish monoplanes with retractable landing gear – Seversky or Spitfire type, according to the official report (almost certainly Morane-Saulnier MS.406s). A pair of I-153s made a high-speed attack, which forced the enemy aircraft to turn back. Three more I-153s joined the pursuit, and the Soviet pilots reported shooting down five without loss to themselves. The Finnish side admitted losing only one Morane 406 that day, but attributed it to anti-aircraft fire.'

Of course, these brief reports do not reflect the entire pattern of events during the conflict. But taking into account the small number of Finnish aircraft involved, and the 'guerilla' tactics adopted by their pilots, it is clear that the Soviet Polikarpov pilots were hardly in a position to make substantial additions to their personal victory tallies during the Winter War. That was the main reason why the achievements of the most effective looked so modest.

The leading ace to emerge from the campaign was Aleksander Bulaev of I-16-equipped 159th IAP. His record shows that he flew dozens of combat sorties, taking off with his squadron from frozen lakes in Karelia, and shot down at least nine enemy aircraft. In 1941-43 Bulaev increased his score to 15 personal and eight shared victories, plus one observation balloon destroyed. Flying more than 350 combat sorties in the I-16, Yak-1, La-5 and P-40, he was shot down and killed on 17 May 1943.

Capt Petr Petrov was a future ace who would make a handful of claims flying the I-15bis as a squadron commander with 68th IAP, 13th Army

Air Force of the Northwestern Front in the Winter War. During a combat mission on 17 February 1940 he landed his biplane fighter on the frozen surface of Lake Muola-Jarvi under enemy fire in order to rescue a comrade who had made a forced landing. For this exploit Petrov was awarded the title of Hero of the Soviet Union on 7 April 1940. During the Great Patriotic War he commanded 254th IAP, equipped with the I-16, and by November 1941 he had scored about ten personal victories. On the 23rd of that month, however, Maj Petrov was shot down and killed by friendly ground fire near Alekseevka railway station in the Kursk region.

Although still doggedly defending Viipuri, the Finns realised that they could no longer hold off the numerically superior enemy. For example, by the end of the first week of March 1940 the VVS RKKA had close to 2000 aircraft committed to the Winter War, whilst the Finnish Air Force could field just 196 – the latter had acquired 140 fighters and bombers from sympathetic countries such as Britain, France and Sweden during the conflict. On 13 March an armistice was signed between Finland and the USSR that saw the former cede a large portion of the Karelian Isthmus and other tracts of land to the Soviets.

Although the Kremlin had achieved the territory it desired, this had come at a great cost in terms of men and materiel. In the air, the VVS RKKA had lost 261 aircraft and 321 men, although its fighter units had in turn claimed 362 Finnish aircraft destroyed. The latter figure was, of course, wildly exaggerated.

To conclude this chapter it should be noted that no specific camouflage schemes were applied to VVS RKKA fighters during the Winter War. Unusually, however, some of the I-15bis and I-16 fighters of 13th OIAE of 61st AB, Baltic Fleet Air Force, were decorated with propaganda slogans such as 'For Communism!', 'For the All-Russian Communist Party of Bolsheviks!', 'For Victory!', 'For the Constitution of the USSR!' and 'Liberty to the oppressed!' However, the hastily painted letters suggest that these inscriptions did not reflect the feelings of the pilots flying these aircraft. It is probable that the application of these slogans was a relatively rare event.

With the Winter War over and the spring sunshine warming their faces, pilots from 13th OIAE look far more relaxed in this informal photograph taken during the summer of 1940. The nearest I-16 Type 17 lacks the recesses for the removable skis in the lower part of its engine cowling – a feature of fighters produced in 1938. The muzzles of the ShVAK 20 mm cannon have been sealed with fabric covers to protect the barrels from dust

This I-16 Type 5 of 13th OIAE bore the legend *For Communism!* A number of aircraft from this unit received patriotic slogans such as this during the campaign

GREAT PATRIOTIC WAR

When the Great Patriotic War erupted on 22 June 1941, the air forces of the Soviet Union's western military districts had a total inventory of 4226 aircraft. Some 1635 of these were I-16s of all variants fielded by 57 fighter regiments distributed across the military districts in frontier areas as follows:

Military District	Number of I-16s
Leningrad Military District Air Force	396
Baltic Military District Air Force	142
Western Special Military District Air Force	361 (or 424 according to other sources)
Kiev Special Military District Air Force	455
Odessa Military District Air Force	143

Air force units of the Northern, Baltic and Black Sea Fleets were also concentrated in the western part of the Soviet Union, and they were able to deploy a total of 763 fighters, including 344 I-16s of all variants.

The Pacific Fleet Air Force had 155 I-16 fighters, with a further 110 operated by naval flying schools as well as 145 UTI-4 trainers. The following table breaks down the geographical distribution of Naval Air Force I-16s;

I-16 variant	Baltic Fleet Air Force	Black Sea Fleet Air Force	Northern Fleet Air Force	Pacific Fleet Air Force	River Flotillas Air Force	Flying Schools & Other Units
I-16 M-22	-	-	-	-	-	26
I-16 Type 5	38	39	-	74	9	67
I-16 Type 10	10	9	-	16	-	17
I-16 Type 12	-	-	-	10	-	-
I-16 Type 17	28	5	-	15	-	-
I-16 Type 18	15	16	-	-	-	-
I-16 Type 24	33	43	16	33	10	4
I-16 Type 27	5	-	-	-	-	-
I-16 Type 28	6	21	-	7	1	-
I-16 Type 29	45	15	-	-	9	2
UTI-2	-	-	-	-	-	3
UTI-4	28	21	2	26	6	62

Air force units deployed along the western border in June 1941 also had around 1300 I-153s at their disposal, and they were distributed as follows;

PLEASE NOTE:

*If your rent account is in credit, Solihull Metropolitan Borough Council will redirect this credit to any other account you may have which is in arrears, in the order of Rent Arrears, Housing Benefit Overpayments, Former Tenancy Arrears, Court Costs and Rechargeable Repairs. This will happen unless we receive alternative instructions from you.

Military District	Number of I-153s	Fighter Regiments
Leningrad Military District Air Force	179	7th, 19th, 26th, 153rd and 154th IAPs
Baltic Military District Air Force	284	15th, 21st, 38th, 42nd, 49th and 148th IAPs
Western Special Military District Air Force	241	122nd, 123rd, 127th and 129th IAPs
Kiev Special Military District Air Force	454	12th, 20th, 23rd, 46th, 91st, 92nd, 149th, 164th and 165th IAPs
Odessa Military District Air Force	143	4th and 55th IAPs

With additional I-153s flown by 61st, 62nd, 66th, 74th, 241st and 299th ShAPs (*Shturmovoy Aviatsionniy Polk* – Attack Air Regiments), 1500 *Chaykas* were based in the western military districts, where they represented more than a third of the fighter strength. I-153s were also operated by the air forces of the Baltic, North and Black Sea Fleets as follows (on 6 June 1941) – Baltic Fleet Air Force, 108 I-153 fighters in 12th, 13th and 104th OIAEs and 71st IAP; Black Sea Fleet Air Force, 73 (or 76) I-153s in 8th, 9th and 32nd IAPs; Northern Fleet Air Force, 18 I-153s in 72nd SAP. Other I-153s were operated by flying schools, units of the inland military districts and regiments based in the Far East, most of which would eventually go into action in the west.

Despite its obsolescence, the I-15bis was still very much in frontline service as both a fighter and ground attack platform within frontier military districts as follows;

Military District	Number of I-15bis fighter aircraft	Number of I-153 and I-15bis ground attack aircraft
Leningrad Military District Air Force	98	72
Baltic Military District Air Force	57	88
Western Special Military District Air Force	15	62
Kiev Special Military District Air Force	77	75
Odessa Military District Air Force	21	-

At daybreak on 22 June 1941 the Wehrmacht advanced across the entire length of the Soviet western frontier from the northern to the southern coastlines. Almost simultaneously the Luftwaffe struck the 66 advanced airfields where most of the VVS RKKA's aircraft were based. These attacks left about 900 Soviet aircraft destroyed on the ground, with follow up strikes raising this figure to a staggering 1200 by nightfall.

The main German assault, delivered by Army Group Centre and supported by the Luftwaffe's *Luftflotte* 2, was directed against the Western Special Military District. The latter lost 738 aircraft on the first day, with 528 being destroyed on the ground and 210 shot down – almost half its operational strength. By inflicting such losses the key objective of the German plan of attack had been achieved. The Luftwaffe now enjoyed complete air superiority over the frontline.

The Germans consolidated their gains over the next few days as Soviet losses continued to mount. During this early phase of the campaign the I-16 units were key targets for the Luftwaffe, and after 48 hours of combat only 937 examples were left from the 1635 that had existed on 21 June.

By 30 June the I-16 inventory of western frontline units had dwindled to 873, of which 99 required repairs to return them to airworthiness.

Despite the sudden onslaught and the severe losses inflicted, I-16 and I-153 pilots were able to oppose the attackers on the first day of the invasion. For example, at 0330 hrs on 22 June I-16s of 33rd IAP took off from Pruzhany airfield. When they returned their pilots reported shooting down six aircraft near Brest. In the Baltic Military District, pilots of 21st and 15th IAP claimed nine victories, while those of 10th IAP reported scoring seven. In the Odessa Military District, Beltry-based 55th IAP reported ten victories and 67th IAP at Bolgrad claimed to have shot down 15 German aircraft by the end of the opening day.

Along the right flank of the frontline in the Western Special Military District, regiments of 11th SAD – 122nd IAP, with 75 I-16s and I-153s at Skidel airfield, and 127th IAP with 72 I-153s at Avgustov, southeast of Grodno – were judged to be both well coordinated and prepared for any attack. At dawn pilots from the division were scrambled to intercept the incoming bombers. Any aircraft requiring repair were left on the ground, where they were destroyed by the Luftwaffe, while all the others engaged the attackers. On its first mission 122nd IAP shot down four aircraft, while 127th IAP first encountered the enemy over the Cherlena-Mosty-Grodno defensive line. After battling against a large formation of German aircraft, its pilots reported shooting down seven for the loss of four I-153s.

All day long German aircraft attacked the airfields of 11th SAD, approaching in groups of up to 30 aircraft. The battles raged until dusk, with 122nd and 127th IAPs claiming to have accounted for 35 aircraft. Lt S Zhukovskiy, who was a 127th IAP squadron commander, flew nine sorties during the day and claimed four aircraft destroyed, as did the regiment's Andrey Danilov. Indeed, the latter pilot fought nine Bf 110s and shot down two before running out of ammunition. He then rammed a third with his *Chayka* – his was just one of ten such *Taran* attacks made by fighter pilots on 22 June. Two SB bomber pilots also rammed German aircraft. Finally, 127th IAP deputy squadron commander A Artemov also shot down three aircraft via more conventional means in nine encounters.

Fellow Western Special Military District regiment 123rd IAP almost certainly produced the first VVS RKKA ace of the conflict when Ivan Kalabushkin claimed a Bf 109, two Ju 88s and two He 111s destroyed during three sorties in his I-153. Subsequently transferred to 362nd and then 11th IAPs (the latter unit defending Moscow), he claimed an early Soviet night victory on 22/23 July when he downed a Do 215, followed by an He 111 eight days later. These were Kalabushkin's final kills with the I-153.

Although Western Special Military District pilots clearly managed to get amongst the Luftwaffe formations sent to knock out their bases, they also suffered the heaviest losses on the first day of the war, both in terms of aircraft destroyed and pilots killed. Indeed, many of the Soviet fighters and bombers in this sector of the frontline were destroyed in the first wave of German strikes. Some units located further east were spared the worst of the onslaught, however. Amongst the latter was 43rd IAD, commanded by Spanish Civil War ace Maj Gen Zakharov, which was deployed at Mogilev and Orsha airfields, and included the following aircraft on strength;

This photograph of a lone I-153 *Chayka* hastily scrambling to confront the enemy was typical of those taken during the summer of 1941, when the VVS RKKA struggled to repel the marauding Luftwaffe as the Wehrmacht pushed further east into the USSR

43rd IAD	**Strength**
160th IAP	60 (or 66, data varies) I-153s and 72 pilots
161st IAP	62 (or 64) I-16s and 70 pilots
162nd IAP	54 I-16s and 75 pilots
163rd IAP	59 I-16s and 72 pilots

The 175 I-16s represented the division's main striking force, and following the disastrous losses suffered on the morning of 22 June they would, for the time being, constitute the backbone of Soviet fighter resistance to the German onslaught. On the first day of the war in the East, 43rd IAD's four regiments had been given their combat assignments and sent west to meet the invaders. Its most successful regiment was 163th IAP, which, jointly with 160th IAP, was assigned to cover Minsk. 163rd's pilots achieved several victories on 22 June, but they did even better on the 24th, claiming 21 aircraft destroyed. This, according to Maj Gen Zakharov, easily exceeded the entire division's score for that day.

One of 43rd IAD's first kills had in fact been credited to Zakharov himself, who, despite his high rank, continued to see combat. He recalled;

'Large twin-engined aircraft were flying over Minsk at low altitude. As I approached them I had no idea that they were Ju 88s. They just kept on flying, and bombed their selected target buildings. There were no enemy fighters anywhere around. After the continuous day-long waves of bombing raids on the city, and having reduced the local airfield to ashes, the Junkers pilots obviously felt completely safe by the evening.

'I was far above them when I saw one approaching the district HQ building in the central city area. I made a diving approach behind it and fired several long bursts of machine gun fire, but the Ju 88 refused to burn – it just banked away and crashed near Minsk's opera house. I then followed the other enemy bomber over the city and set him on fire. He left the area trailing smoke. I couldn't wait to see him crash, but I'm sure the Ju 88 couldn't survive. Just like his comrade, he was at very low altitude.'

Zakharov carried on flying regular combat missions over the next few days, although it was not until early October that he celebrated another victory. This time his victim was an Hs 126 reconnaissance aircraft intercepted over the Yukhnov-Medyn highway. A few days later, on 20 October, Zakharov was relieved of his command for refusing to comply with an order to transfer his division to Gzhatsk. His dismissal was not rescinded, despite almost immediate proof that he had been right – the airfield at Gzhatsk was overrun by German forces just hours after the transfer order had been received. The disgraced general was appointed to command a flying school at Ulan-Ude, and it would take a year of continuous lobbying before he was able to return to active service.

In December 1942 Zakharov was appointed commander of 303rd IAD, one of whose subordinate units would achieve fame as the Normandie-Nieman French volunteer regiment. By May 1945 the division had become subordinated to the 1st Air Army of the 3rd Byelorussian Front, and Zakharov had flown 153 combat sorties, fought in 48 aerial combats and shot down ten enemy aircraft. On 19 April 1945 he was awarded the title of Hero of the Soviet Union. In three wars Zakharov had scored 18 individual and four shared victories. Post-war, Grigoriy Zakharov continued his service in the higher echelons of the Air Force and, according to his memoirs, he retained his personal Yak-3 fighter so that he could maintain his flying proficiency into the 1950s.

TARAN

In the desperate days of June 1941 many Soviet pilots sacrificed their lives to help stem the aerial assault by ramming German aircraft in *Taran* attacks, often after they had exhausted their supply of ammunition. One of the first was Lt Alexandr Moklyak of 67th IAP, who, having shot down his fourth enemy aircraft on 22 June, despatched his fifth to become an ace when he rammed a Ju 88 – the third Junkers bomber he had destroyed. This final attack cost Moklyak his life. Fellow I-16 pilot Lt Vasiliy Loboda of 19th IAP also rammed an aircraft after claiming two previously shot down. Future ace Nikolay Ignatyev of 728th IAP was also credited with his first victory via a ramming attack on the 22nd.

These attacks might represent a last desperate resort that came to be regarded as acts of supreme heroism, but during the first few days of the war many pilots were so determined to stop the invasion that they willingly embraced such methods. Others may have followed their examples in the heat of battle or when they had used up all their ammunition. Whatever the reason, on 22 June alone 15 Soviet pilots brought down enemy aircraft in ramming attacks, and many more would choose a similar path to success. In the desperate environment of 1941 pilots were even encouraged to make such sacrifices.

They did not go unrecognised. The first wartime pilots nominated for the title Hero of the Soviet Union were all selected from a shortlist of aviators who had brought down enemy aircraft by ramming them.

Taran was also a tactic wholeheartedly adopted over Leningrad, where the fighting was particularly severe. Pilots from 153rd, 154th and 158th IAPs were amongst the most successful practitioners of this high-risk combat tactic, and on 27 June future ace Jnr Lt Petr Kharitonov of 158th IAP rammed a Ju 88 with his I-16 near Pskov – he would claim an He 111 using the same method on 25 August. Jnr Lts Stepan Zdorovtsev and Mikhail Zhukov, also from 158th IAP, would follow his example on 28 June when they too downed bombers with their I-16s. On all three occasions the pilots involved were flying their first combat sorties, and they had made their attacks after their guns had jammed or they had run out of ammunition. They were all able to force land their damaged I-16s.

The commander of the Northern (Leningrad) Front Air Force, Air Marshal A Novikov, later offered his own perspective on these events;

'A day or two after Zdorovtsev's and Zhukov's ram attacks I reported to the Northern Front commander, M Popov, and to A Zhdanov (the Communist Party leader in charge of Leningrad's defence) about these three heroes and suggested their nomination as Heroes of the Soviet Union. Later in the day I was present when Zhdanov reported their feats of bravery to Joseph Stalin over the telephone. Stalin supported our recommendation. No paperwork pertaining to this matter has been found in any archives because there were no documents. It was a telephone conversation between Zhdanov and Stalin, and the resulting telegram to HQ substituted for formal documentation in those days.'

On 8 July 1941 the Presidium of the Supreme Soviet of the USSR issued an order to award the title to Kharitonov, Zdorovtsev and Zhukov.

158th IAP I-16 pilot, and future ace, Jnr Lt Petr Kharitonov made a successful ramming attack on a Ju 88 near Pskov on 27 June 1941. He would claim an He 111 using the same method on 25 August. Severely wounded in combat in September 1941, Kharitonov did not return to active service until 1944. From then until the end of the war he served with fighter units of the air defence forces, claiming a total of 14 enemy aircraft destroyed

The wartime careers of the three pilots differed dramatically. Stepan Zdorovtsev was killed in combat on 9 July 1941. On 3 September I-16 pilots Mikhail Zhukov and his wingman P Shestakov shot down a Bf 110. Later in the year Zhukov converted to the P-40E, and 158th IAP records indicate that on 3 December he shot down two enemy aircraft over Lake Ladoga's Cape Osinovets. For his subsequent performance against the Finnish landing force he was awarded the Order of Combat Red Banner. On 12 January 1943, during the initial stage of the Leningrad breakout, Zhukov, now a senior lieutenant with 158th IAP, was killed in action. He had flown 286 combat sorties and fought in 66 aerial engagements, during which he scored nine individual and five shared victories.

Finally, Petr Kharitonov was severely wounded during September 1941 and would not return to active service until 1944. From then until war's end he served with fighter units of the air defence forces, claiming a total of 14 enemy aircraft destroyed.

DEFENDING MOSCOW

Within a month of the initial attack on 22 June the rapid German penetration of the USSR had placed Luftwaffe bomber units within range of Moscow. The VVS RKKA responded by forming 6th IAK (*Istrebitelniy Aviatsionniy Korpus* – Fighter Aviation Corps) of the air defence forces, which by 31 July had a strength of 495 fighters, including 106 I-16s. The latter were distributed across the following regiments and airfields – 16th IAP, with eight I-16s at Lubertsy; 34th IAP, with 30 I-16s at Vnukovo; 27th IAP, with 31 I-16s at Klin; 176th IAP, with 15 I-16s at Stepykhino; 233rd IAP, with 18 I-16s at Tushino; and 2nd OIAE, with four I-16s at Ramenskoe.

By 15 August German bombers had made 18 night raids on Moscow, but they had failed to do any tangible damage to the Soviet capital thanks to the efforts of the air defence forces. During these tense days and nights Soviet pilots continued to make ram attacks, including 177th IAP pilot Snr Lt Viktor Talalikhin. Patrolling over Podolsk at 15,000 ft in his I-16 on the night of 7 August, he had spotted an He 111 below him. Using up all of his ammunition as he chased the bomber down to a lower altitude, Talalikhin closed on the aircraft and attempted to ram it. He was wounded in the right arm by defensive fire, however, although he eventually succeeded in badly damaging the He 111's tail, causing it to spin into the ground. With his I-16 badly damaged, Talalikhin was forced to bail out.

The next morning Talalikhin found himself the first major aerial hero of the war to the Soviet people in the wake of his successful night *Taran* attack. He became a Hero of the Soviet Union two days later. Parts of the rammed He 111 are still on display at the Central Museum of Armed Forces in Moscow. A veteran of the Winter War, where he had claimed three kills, Talalikhin shot a Ju 88 down the day before his ramming attack. His final two kills came on 27 October 1941, when he destroyed a pair of Bf 109s over Podolsk before falling victim to a third fighter.

Meanwhile, near Murmansk, on the northernmost segment of the Soviet-German frontline, 145th IAP was the largest fighter unit in the region. Part of the 14th Army of the Karelian Front, the regiment was equipped with 56 I-16s, and many of its pilots were veterans of the Soviet-Finnish Winter War. And it was the Polikarpov pilots who had to

Jnr Lt Mikhail Zhukov, also of 158th IAP, performed a successful ramming attack on a German bomber on 28 June 1941. By the time he was shot down and killed on 12 January 1943 during the initial stages of the Leningrad breakout, Zhukov had flown a total of 286 combat sorties and fought in 66 aerial engagements, scoring nine individual and five shared victories

withstand the fiercest fighting of the initial phase of the new conflict. The most successful during the first months of the war were Winter War veterans Leonid Galchenko and Viktor Mironov.

A squadron commander, Galchenko shot down seven enemy aircraft in three months and was nominated for the title of Hero of the Soviet Union. By the time he actually received it, on 6 June 1942, his score had risen to nine individual and 12 shared victories. Galchenko's most famous mission in the I-16 came on 15 September 1941 when he led five Polikarpovs against a force of 30 bombers, four of which were claimed destroyed without loss. He initially flew the I-16 Type 10, but in the autumn his unit converted to the LaGG-3. In mid-1942 Galchenko was promoted to command 609th IAP. During the war he flew 410 combat sorties, fought in 90 aerial battles and was credited with 24 individual and 12 shared kills. He was a divisional commander by war's end.

Snr Lt Viktor Mironov was Galchenko's wingman during the latter half of 1941, and he had flown 127 operational sorties and shot down five enemy aircraft in 25 combats by the end of September – he claimed one of the Ju 88s downed on the 15th of that month. Mironov followed Galchenko to 609th IAP in the autumn of 1942. A veteran of 356 sorties, and with ten individual and 15 shared victories to his name, Mironov was killed in a flying accident on 16 February 1943.

Arguably the most famous fighter unit in the north was I-16-equipped 72nd SAP of the Northern Fleet, based at Vaenga airfield. Its leading ace during 1941-42 was Boris Safonov, who proved to be the most effective fighter pilot on the Northern Front during the first year of the war. A pre-war I-15 pilot with many flying hours (but no actual combat) to his credit, Safonov later became regimental commander, while 72nd SAP was re-designated 2nd GSAP in January 1942 following its success.

The first four I-16 Type 24s had arrived at 72nd SAP's base in April 1941, where they had been extensively used for training. The regiment was still primarily equipped with the I-15bis when Germany invaded, although squadron commander Snr Lt Safonov used one of just three I-16s on strength in his unit to down his first Ju 88 on 24 June. Flying six

177th IAP pilot Jnr Lt Viktor Talalikhin (second from left) discusses a recent action in the defence of Moscow with his comrades in the summer of 1941. He became the first major aerial hero of the war to the Soviet people in the wake of his successful night *Taran* attack on an He 111 on 7 August 1941, Talalikhin receiving the title of Hero of the Soviet Union for his act of bravery. A veteran of the Winter War, Talalikhin's final victories came on 27 October 1941, when he destroyed a pair of Bf 109s over Podolsk before falling victim to a third German fighter or seven sorties per day during the first weeks of the war, Safonov regularly claimed both individual and shared victories over a variety of Luftwaffe aircraft. He enjoyed particular success against German bombers, leading nine I-16s against a large formation on 7 July that saw the Soviet pilots claim ten destroyed without loss. Safonov was credited with two bombers destroyed one week later, followed by a pair of Ju 88s on 27 July to give him ace status. A further 13 bombers were claimed over Murmansk on 9 August, one of which (a Ju 88) was downed by Safonov, along with two other unidentified types. By the end of the month he had flown 150 sorties and claimed 13 individual and three shared victories.

In early July 1941 the military photographer Khaldey took a picture of Safonov standing beside an I-16 displaying the legend *'For Stalin!'* painted on the fuselage, and it was assumed that this was his personal aircraft. Indeed, propaganda slogans were applied to all three I-16s of 72nd IAP in late June following the invasion. One bore the slogans *'For All-Russian Communist Party of Bolsheviks!'* and *'Death To Fascists!'*, while the fighter flown by fellow ace Snr Lt Aleksander Kovalenko had also received the legend *'For Stalin!'*, as well as *'For Communism!'*. Finally, the I-16 flown by Sgt Surzhenko bore the slogan *'For the USSR!'*.

Boris Safonov may have flown all three fighters between 26 June and 10 July 1941, as well as several of the 22 newer I-16 Type 24s and 28s that had been hastily delivered to 72nd SAP at around this time. Documents show that from 10 July to 3 October 1941 Safonov usually flew cannon-armed I-16 construction number 2821z95, but there is no evidence to suggest that it displayed any slogans on its fuselage. His last reported I-16 sortie came on 15 September 1941, when he shot down a Bf 110, a Ju 87 and an Hs 126. The next day Safonov, now CO of 72nd IAP, was awarded the title of Hero of the Soviet Union. He subsequently flew Hurricanes supplied under Lend-Lease and, from January 1942, P-40Es.

On 30 May 1942 Lt Col Safonov took off on his 224th, and last, mission. His objective was to provide air cover for convoy PQ-16, which was approaching Murmansk. A flight of three P-40Es led by Safonov attacked six enemy bombers approaching the ships. Safonov shot down two Ju 88s but he was forced to ditch in the sea when his engine stopped. The convoy's guard ships screened the area but failed to find him. His logbook survived to show a complete list of his confirmed kills –

Press photographer Khaldey takes an official picture of Boris Safonov, squadron commander of 72nd SAP of the Northern Fleet Air Force, at Vaenga airfield with an I-16 displaying the legend *For Stalin!* painted on the fuselage. The construction number of the I-16 (24P2189) is just visible on the fighter's vertical stabiliser. Safonov was the leading ace on the Northern Front during the first year of the war

20 individual and six shared, most of which were scored flying the I-16.

China War veteran Dmitriy Kudymov was serving as a squadron commander with I-16-equipped 9th IAP of the Black Sea Fleet Air Force when Germany attacked in June 1941. His unit was based near Ochakov and charged with defending the 'Marti' shipbuilding works in nearby Nikolaev. In addition to their air defence duties, 9th IAP fighters were also employed on ground attack missions. When Soviet troops abandoned Odessa to the invaders the survivors of 9th IAP were relocated to Eysk for retraining, as Kudymov recalled;

'I arrived in Eysk in late August 1941 with the rank of major. We didn't have much time for conversion training as fighters were badly needed at the front. The new aircraft were not welcome. The MiG-1 fighters delivered to my squadron were too heavy in flight and too slow to climb. Moreover, they demonstrated a much wider radius of turn compared to the nimble I-16 "Swallows" which we had previously flown in combat.'

Kudymov later joined 7th IAP in the Sebastopol area, which was equipped with newer MiG-3s. He remained here until mid-1942, when, after falling out with his squadron's commissar, he became a ferry pilot flying replacement aircraft to frontline units. In November of that year Kudymov was made CO of 13th OIAE of the Baltic Sea Fleet Air Force;

'The squadron was comprised of 12 combat aircraft divided into four flights, and it was based at Grazhdanka airfield in the city of Leningrad. We had several versions of the I-16 on strength, and by then the pilots had invented a new nickname for the Polikarpov fighter. Instead of "Swallow" they called it "Ishak" (Ass). From their predecessors the new "asses" had inherited excellent manoeuvrability and high speed. I fell in love with what I regarded to be the perfect combat aeroplane.'

13th OIAE was among the last to swap its I-16s for newer fighter types. In the summer of 1943 its pilots escorted Il-2 ground attack aircraft of 57th ShAP of the Baltic Fleet and Pe-2 dive-bombers of 12th BAP commanded by Vasiliy Rakov. Kudymov's confirmed aerial victories with the I-16 during this period included one over a Bf 109 near Mustolovo. The 13th performed effectively in the Leningrad theatre for more than a year, suffering only a handful of losses in return.

On 23 February 1944 Kudymov led a group of six I-16s of the 3rd Detached Fighter Air Regiment providing cover for five Il-2s of the 57th ShAP led by Capt Klimenko, which was raiding enemy positions near the village of Pokrovskoe. On their way back the I-16s were attacked by nine enemy fighters, and Kudymov shot one down. As it crashed in Soviet-held territory, the victory was confirmed by ground troops. Kudymov's victim turned out to be an Fw 190 displaying 29 victory symbols on its rudder. This combat was among the last involving the I-16. In February 1944 13th OIAE transferred to 21st IAP of the Baltic Fleet Air Force and re-equipped with the Yak-7 and later the Yak-9D. By war's end Lt Col Dmitriy Kudymov's score stood at 12 personal and 29 shared victories.

N Khromov of 12th OIAE, Baltic Fleet Air Force, poses in the cockpit of an I-153 in 1943 in the Leningrad area. The aircraft displays 11 victory stars on its fuselage (ten visible in this photograph), although not all the kills represented were officially confirmed, for according to available sources Khromov's tally was three individual and four shared victories

An I-16 Type 24 is prepared for a combat sortie, possibly on the Leningrad Front. The fighter, which has been armed with six RS-82 rocket projectiles, is having its engine oil topped up. The I-16 is parked in a permanent shelter adorned with the stirring legend 'All our forces are aimed at defeating the enemy!'

ODESSA FRONT

In the Odessa area on the southern sector of the frontline pilots of 69th IAP of the Independent Black Sea Army Air Force flew their I-16s with success in 1941. The regiment was commanded by Spanish Civil War veteran Maj Lev Shestakov. He had arrived in Spain as a lieutenant in August 1937, and by the following April he had been credited with shooting down a Bf 109 and a

CR.32, and sharing in the destruction of a second Bf 109. Some sources, however, put his score in Spain at eight aircraft shot down. Upon his return to the Soviet Union, Shestakov was awarded the Order of Lenin and the Order of Combat Red Banner.

During the defence of Odessa in 1941, Shestakov claimed three more individual and eight shared victories over enemy aircraft. On 10 February 1942 he became a Hero of the Soviet Union, and the following July he was appointed commander of 9th GIAP, which was specially tasked with securing air superiority over Stalingrad. Only those pilots who had at least five individual victories to their credit could be considered suitable for the unit. A year later Shestakov was made CO of 6th GIAD, but shortly afterwards he found himself leading 19th IAP. This was the first elite fighter unit specially formed by Air Marshal A Novikov, commander of the VVS RKKA, and its sole mission was 'free hunting'.

According to Red Army Air Force documentation, Lev Shestakov had flown more than 200 missions by January 1944. In 82 aerial engagements he achieved 15 individual and 11 shared kills prior to his death in combat on 13 March 1944, by which time he had been promoted to the rank of colonel. Shestakov's total score, including his service in Spain, had risen to 23 individual and 44 shared victories in more than 400 combat missions.

BALTIC ACES 1941-43

The most effective I-16 and I-153-equipped fighter units during World War 2 were almost certainly those of the Baltic Fleet Air Force. At the outbreak of war it controlled 61st IAB (*Istrebitelniy Aviatsionniy Brigada – Fighter Aviation Brigade*), based at Nizino, Lipovo, Kummelovo and Kuplya airfields. 5th IAP (77 I-16s, two I-153s, 16 I-15bis and 13 MiG-3s), 12th OIAE (12 I-16s, 30 I-153s and three I-15bis) and 13th OIAE (25 I-16s and 12 I-15bis) flew from these bases. 10th Combined Air Brigade was also assigned to the Baltic Fleet Air Force, flying from Tallinn, Hanko, Kerstovo and Pernov. Its units were 13th (38 I-16s and 12 I-153s) and 71st IAPs (52 I-153s and three I-15bis).

13th IAP, led by Lt Col I Romanenko, comprised four squadrons – 1st Squadron equipped with I-16 Type 17s, 2nd Squadron with I-16 Type 24s, 27s and 29s, 3rd Squadron with I-16 Type 5s and 4th Squadron with I-153s. At the beginning of the war 13th IAP's units were scattered over a number of airfields. Some were based at Lagsberg near Tallinn, and it was from here on 25 June that future I-16 ace Capt Aleksey Antonenko achieved his first victory. Indeed, the entire city of Tallinn saw the Ju 88 that he attacked go down. Antonenko was an experienced pilot who had fought in the Khalkhin Gol conflict as well as the Winter War. The Junkers bomber was his first of four individual and six shared kills.

13th IAP's 4th Squadron, equipped with I-153s and led by Capt L Belousov, was based in the Hanko Peninsula when the war commenced. A strip of land 16 miles long and between four and seven miles wide, it had been 'rented' from Finland for 30 years as one of the spoils of the Winter War. When Finland sided with the Germans in the invasion of the USSR, the Hanko Peninsula found itself very much in the frontline.

4th Squadron's naval base was still in the process of construction when it was targeted by Finnish artillery. Some facilities were already in place but others would be hastily completed over the coming weeks under persistent shelling. Aircraft shelters were covered with six to eight layers of tree trunks, which were sufficient to protect the fighters within against even direct hits from shells.

Hanko naval base occupied a strategic position at the mouth of the Gulf of Finland, and it helped Soviet forces control the gulf itself, as well as the southern coastal area of Finland. Although it acted as a 'bottleneck' for Axis forces attempting to enter or exit the gulf, on the other hand, the enemy was well aware of the exact location of almost every facility within the base. Finnish artillery shelled the site continuously and by the time of the German assault on the base, Luftwaffe reconnaissance aircraft had taken detailed photographs of the entire peninsula. As a result the Soviets were to lose many aircraft to enemy artillery fire as they took off and landed.

2 July saw two flights of I-16 Type 17s of 13th IAP ferried to Hanko under the leadership of 1st Squadron CO, Capt Leonovich. Later, more fighters from 13th and 71st IAPs and 13th OIAE arrived too. The defence of Hanko lasted for more than five months, and there were many stories of heroic battles, clear-cut victories and bitter defeats.

On 3 July, future aces Aleksey Antonenko and Petr Brinko (a veteran of the Khalkhin Gol conflict) became the first pilots to be allowed to conduct missions as a pair. The following morning two biplanes appeared from the Finnish side, which ground observers reported as Bulldog fighters. They fired at the Soviet artillery batteries and dropped small bombs, prompting two I-16s to be immediately scrambled from beneath their camouflaged revetments in opposition. Brinko shot down one of the Finnish aircraft for his first kill, while Antonenko chased the other biplane until it had reached the sanctuary provided by Finnish flak.

Four days later Antonenko and Brinko headed for 13th IAP's base at Tallinn, which was 62 miles from Hanko across the Gulf of Finland. En route they shot down a German twin-engined aircraft that they reported as being either a Ju 88 or a Do 17. On 9 July the pair claimed to have destroyed two Finnish fighters that were attempting to attack a nearby torpedo boat base. The following day, Aleksey Lazukin and Konstantin Belorustsev attacked a Finnish airfield in their I-153s, escorted by Antonenko and Brinko. In an engagement with Finnish fighters (either G.50s or D.XXIs) five aircraft were reported to have been shot down by the I-16 aces.

The Baltic pilots' success was soon noticed by their superiors, and on 14 July 1941 Antonenko and Brinko became the first naval pilots

The engine of this I-153 of 71st IAP is about to be fired up with the help of a Hucks starter at Bychye Pole in the summer of 1942

This I-153 of 71st IAP is also being connected to a Hucks starter in the summer of 1942. These aircraft, assigned to No 1 Squadron, which was led by ace Capt Petr Biskup, are equipped with RS-82 rocket projectiles on underwing RO-82 launch rails

An I-16 Type 29 of 13th IAP hastily taxies out from the protection of a multilayer tree-trunk shelter during the bitter defence of the Hanko Peninsula in the summer of 1941

to become Heroes of the Soviet Union. Having been in constant action since the beginning of the month, Antonenko was the first to succumb when, on 25 July, an enemy artillery shell exploded in front of his I-16 as he was landing. The fighter nosed over, throwing its pilot out – Antonenko was killed instantly. He had shot down 11 enemy aircraft prior to his demise.

Twenty-four hours prior to Antonenko's death, Brinko had 'made ace' by ramming a Bf 110, and he claimed one more kill (a Ju 88) over Tallinn in early August before being transferred to Leningrad. Here, he formed a successful partnership with Capt Maltsev, Brinko increasing his personal score to 15 victories.

On the evening of 14 September the Germans launched an observation balloon near Ropsha. Fighters were sent up to destroy it, but the first attack proved to be a failure. Petr Brinko insisted that he could do the job on his own. After take-off, he remained at treetop height in his I-16 as he approached the balloon, before zooming up to fire six RS-82 rockets at the blimp. His target erupted in flames, but Brinko's I-16 was also hit by ground fire. Although the ace was able to bring his badly damaged fighter home, he did not survive the wounds he had suffered during the mission.

One of the most effective Baltic Fleet I-16 pilots was Vasiliy Golubev, who also began his combat career at Hanko with 13th IAP. He soon passed the milestone of 100 combat sorties, which included 45 ground attack missions. Golubev claimed his first kill on 28 June when he downed a Ju 88, and he continued to score regularly over the next six months, downing both German and Finnish aircraft (including two captured I-153s on 24 October that gave him ace status).

A hero of the defence of the naval base in the Hanko Peninsula, Petr Brinko (left) describes a recent combat to his comrades. Having claimed 15 victories, Brinko succumbed to wounds he suffered in combat while downing a German observation balloon on 14 September 1941

A handful of Golubev's victories had been claimed using relatively rare RS-82 rockets, which had made their combat debut with the I-16 in Mongolia in 1939. Despite the weapon proving itself in the Khalkhin Gol conflict, no mass installation had followed, however. Indeed, by mid-1940 only two fighter regiments had a handful of projectile-armed aircraft – seven I-16s of 22nd IAP of the Trans-Baikal Military District at Bain Tumen airfield and 17 I-16s of 24th IAP at Kubinka airfield, near Moscow. Even then, although the fighters had the underwing launch rails they never carried the rockets, leaving the equipment to deteriorate.

On 9 August 1940 the Red Army General Staff issued an order requiring commanders of the Military District Air Forces and the Far Eastern Front to remove rocket-launching equipment from their aircraft. The equipment was to be put into storage and the engineering instructions and manuals withheld, pending further instructions.

Rocket projectiles and launchers continued to be built, however. According to Red Army supply plans, the aircraft factories should by 1 January 1941 have equipped 600 I-16s with RO-82 rails for RS-82 rockets, but only 300 had been delivered to air force units by that date. On 14 April 1941 the Air Force Chief of Administration reported to the Head of the Air Force, P Zhigarev, that 28 1939-built I-16s, 275 1940-built I-16s and 38 1941-built I-16s had been equipped with RO-82 rails. Little had changed by the summer.

This I-16 Type 29, equipped with six RO-82 rocket launchers (but no RS-82 rockets) and two PSB-21 underwing fuel tanks, was photographed during State testing in August 1940. Because of the installation of the launchers, the red star insignia (just visible to left) had to be relocated closer to the wingtips

Pre-war, regular fighter pilots had only the vaguest idea about the new armament, and this is confirmed by many post-war memoirs. Vasiliy Golubev had this to say about Soviet pilot training in the spring of 1941;

'Pilots just kept on improving their knowledge of the I-16 (Types 24, 27 and 29), while the ground-training programme was much less intensive. For several days they did nothing but study the electrical circuitry used to launch the RS-82s. The equipment had been installed on the aircraft, but training in its use was still restricted.'

As detailed later in this chapter, Golubev would soon get to grips with the RS-82 once combat commenced.

On 2 December 1941 Soviet forces finally evacuated Hanko, taking five I-153s and eight I-16s with them to Kronstadt. Golubev continued his service in the Leningrad area, including regular missions over the city's vital transport lifeline, Lake Ladoga. Its frozen surface provided the only access to the besieged city during the winter months, despite regular attacks by the Luftwaffe. Based at Vystav and Novaya Ladoga, 13th IAP would play a major role in defending the 'ice highway'. Indeed, between 12 March and 13 April 1942 its pilots were credited with destroying 54 enemy aircraft for the loss of just two I-16s. The unit's achievements were recognised in mid-March by its re-designation as 4th GIAP.

Winter War veteran Gennadiy Tsokolaev was involved in much of the action during 1941-42. For example, on 19 July 1941 he and another I-16 pilot called Leonovich took off on a reconnaissance mission. During the sortie they were attacked by Finnish fighters, and both

Winter War veteran Snr Lt Gennadiy Tsokolaev addresses young pilots of 4th GIAP at Novaya Ladoga airfield in the spring of 1942. By war's end Tsokolaev had flown an astounding 510 combat sorties, many of them in the I-16

men claimed to have shot down a D.XXI. On 5 November Tsokolaev destroyed a Hawk 75 from Finnish unit LeLv 32. In April 1942 he was made a squadron CO with 4th GIAP, and on 14 June he received the title of Hero of the Soviet Union. During World War 2 Tsokolaev flew 510 combat sorties, resulting in seven individual and 15 shared kills (all with the I-16).

Another pilot to 'make ace' with 13th IAP (4th GIAP) was Mikhail Vasilyev. Having already received the Order of Red Banner for his service in the Soviet-Finnish war, he made a significant contribution to the defence of the Hanko Peninsula, before fighting the enemy over Leningrad. On 14 June 1942 Vasilyev was awarded the title of Hero of the Soviet Union for a service record that included 440 combat sorties, 92 aerial engagements and six individual and 16 shared victories (all with the I-16). On 5 May 1943, as a squadron commander with the 4th GIAP, Mikhail Vasilyev was shot down and killed.

Their engines wrapped in thermal covers to keep out the worst of the cold, these I-16s of 4th GIAP were photographed at Novaya Ladoga airfield in the spring of 1942. The closest I-16 also displays a newly applied Guards symbol on its fuselage. The fighter was flown by Snr Lt Gennadiy Tsokolaev, who claimed seven individual and 15 shared victories with the I-16

Fighting alongside 13th IAP throughout this period was 71st IAP, which was equipped almost exclusively with the I-153 (it also had a few I-15bis on strength too). Although predominantly flying ground attack missions, the regiment also produced a handful of aces, including Konstantin Solovyov. Like many of his contemporaries, he had fought in the Winter War with the Baltic Fleet Air Force. By June 1941 he was a flight commander, although he would soon become a squadron CO. Solovyov scored his first victory on 22 September 1941 when he downed a Ju 88 near Peterhof, west of Leningrad. On 27 March 1942 he was leading a formation of five I-153s in an attack on enemy positions at Hogland Island when they were attacked by three Finnish Hawk 75s and two D.XXIs. The ensuing battle lasted for 20 minutes, during which time Solovyov sent a D.XXI crashing into the gulf east of Hogland Island.

By July 1942, having spent a full year in combat on the Baltic Front, Solovyov had flown 427 sorties, including 110 ground attack and 50 reconnaissance missions. In 65 aerial battles he had achieved four individual and eight shared victories, and had participated in the shooting down of three enemy aircraft at night. On 23 October 1942 Solovyov received the title of Hero of the Soviet Union, and on 17 December he was promoted to become deputy commander of 4th GIAP. Ten days later, however, he was killed in a flying accident.

When the war began Vladimir Abramov was a pilot in the 3rd Squadron of 71st IAP. During his first year with the unit he filled the roles of flight commander, deputy squadron commander and then squadron commander. Abramov achieved his first shared victory in July 1941 when he participated in the destruction of a Ju 88 targeting Riga. He also demonstrated proficiency in aerial reconnaissance, and during one such mission he flew over the Kunda-Kohtla-Järve defensive line and spotted

An I-15bis of 71st IAP, Baltic Fleet Air Force, flown by ace Vladimir Abramov takes off from an airfield near Leningrad during the summer of 1941. It is uncertain whether he claimed any of his victories with the elderly Polikarpov fighter

German troops preparing to cut off Tallinn. Among other aircraft types, Abramov flew a captured Hs 126 when conducting these hazardous reconnaissance missions.

Although the feat is not officially acknowledged, Abramov helped bring down an Fw 200 Condor near Ülemiste railway station in July 1941, the aircraft's demise being reported by ground observers. The Condor was initially attacked and damaged by Abramov and then finished off by 13th IAP aces Antonenko and Brinko. On 18 August, while flying an I-15bis, Abramov downed a Bf 110 and badly damaged a second *Zerstörer*. Two more victories followed on 10 September. His personal record showed that between 22 June 1941 and 22 April 1942 he flew 308 sorties, including 70 ground attack and 87 reconnaissance missions, and shared in the destruction of nine aircraft. He also achieved two kills. On 22 July 1944 Abramov became a Hero of the Soviet Union, and by war's end he had flown 600 sorties, fought in 67 aerial engagements and accounted for 29 aircraft, either individually or shared.

Another 71st IAP pilot who deserves special mention is regimental commissar Ivan Serbin, who later became commissar of 61st IAB. During the summer of 1942 the Luftwaffe made a series of massive raids on Kronstadt naval base, which was defended by the 20 I-153s and I-16s of 71st IAP. From 28 May to 14 July the Germans lost 24 aircraft in that area, yet 71st IAP sustained no losses. Four of the aircraft downed were He 111s credited to Commissar Serbin flying an I-153 – he claimed three individually and shared in the destruction of the fourth. One such kill came at dusk on 3 June when Serbin was patrolling at 3250 ft. Sighting a Heinkel bomber, he fired RS-82 rockets at it. The He 111 crashed into Puhtola Hill and exploded. Returning to his patrol area near Kotlin Island, Serbin sighted another bomber and downed it too. The He 111 hit the water in sight of the Kronstadt garrison.

Serbin was just one of a number of Polikarpov pilots in the Baltic Fleet Air Force to make extensive use of rockets during the initial phase of the war. Fellow 71st IAP ace Aleksander Baturin, for example, scored several victories with his RS-82-equipped I-153. He achieved his first victory on 21 August 1941 when he shot down a Ju 88 near Tallinn, but in a subsequent combat shell splinters injured his right eye. In a letter to his family, dated 17 February 1942, Baturin wrote;

'In general I'm okay, apart from my sore eye and the splinters in the bridge of my nose. I have to fly in tinted glasses. It's hard to cope, but I have to fight. So despite only

Ivan Serbin, Commissar of 71st IAP of the Baltic Sea Air Force, congratulates I-153 pilot Snr Lt Vladimir Abramov of the regiment's 3rd Squadron following a successful mission during the late summer of 1941. Serbin's score with the I-16 and I-153 was five individual and three shared victories, while Vladimir Abramov achieved ten individual and 15 shared victories in Polikarpov fighters

An I-153 of 71st IAP is rolled out of its unusually camouflaged shelter on the Leningrad Front during the winter of 1941-42

having an eye-and-a-half I've already shot down five of the vultures. Well, we must win the war first and then I'll take care of my eye.'

On 3 April 1942, during the massive German air raid on Kronstadt naval base, Baturin's group of eight I-153s attacked the enemy bombers with RS-82s. Having broken up the formation, the I-153s doggedly attacked the aircraft, and Baturin claimed three shot down. Later that same day he claimed another bomber destroyed to round off a day's work that earned him the Order of Combat Red Banner. A few days later Baturin downed three more aircraft in an engagement over Leningrad.

By June 1942 Snr Lt Baturin was a deputy squadron commander with 71st IAP, having completed 421 sorties, including 67 reconnaissance missions. He had also shot down nine enemy aircraft in 81 aerial engagements, and was counted as being among the most experienced of Soviet fighter pilots. On 23 October 1942 Baturin became a Hero of the Soviet Union, and by war's end he was credited with 18 individual and 12 shared victories. He had flown 563 combat sorties and fought in 94 aerial engagements. Baturin stayed in the Naval Air Force post-war.

This I-153 was also assigned to 71st IAP of the Baltic Fleet Air Force, and it was photographed taxiing out before taking off from Lavensaari in August 1942. Note the non-standard finish to the black and green camouflage on its uppersurfaces

NIGHTFIGHTER

The Luftwaffe attacked Leningrad around the clock in 1941-42, which in turn meant that Polikarpov fighters also sortied after dark in an attempt to defend the beleaguered city. One of the most successful nightfighter pilots during this period was I-16 squadron commander Snr Lt Vasiliy Matsievich of 26th IAP, assigned to 7th IAK of the Air Defence Forces. A veteran of the Winter War, he was involved in so many interceptions of night raids on the city during the autumn of 1941 that Air Marshal A Novikov

devoted two chapters of his book *In the Leningrad Sky* to Matsievich and his nocturnal exploits. One account described a night duel involving Matsievich and an He 111 on 26 October, Novikov writing that 'The Heinkel was downed over Leningrad. It went up like a flying ammunition dump, illuminating the entire city'. Matsievich had been patrolling the Gulf of Finland west of Leningrad when, after 45 minutes in the air, he sighted the bomber's engine exhausts. Fearing that he might lose his quarry in thick cloud, Matsievich immediately launched six rockets at the He 111 from behind and below. All six hit the Heinkel, which exploded.

By June 1942 Matsievich had flown 196 combat sorties and fought in 44 aerial battles. He had also scored 16 individual and six shared victories, all with the I-16. On 14 February 1943 he became a Hero of the Soviet Union, and was later promoted to command his regiment, which was subsequently re-designated 26th GIAP. Matsievich stayed in the Air Force until 1964, retiring with the rank of colonel. His wartime record included about 250 combat sorties and participation in 64 aerial combats. He also shot down 24 enemy aircraft.

Matsievich's destruction of the He 111 as detailed above clearly revealed the effectiveness of the RS-82 rocket when used at close range on a large target. However, as previously noted in this chapter, pre-war doubts over the weapon's lethality resulted in a reluctance by the VVS RKKA to wholeheartedly embrace the RS-82 as an effective weapon for its Polikarpov fighters, despite it being widely available. This in turn meant that many units had to hastily install the launchers literally 'under fire' in the field, often months after the outbreak of the war.

For example, in the Sebastopol area commanders did not consider using the RS-82 until as late as November 1941, when the Black Sea Fleet Air Force was being re-deployed to a new airfield in Nizhniy Chorgun. Future ace Konstantin Denisov of 8th IAP, who fought in the defence of Sebastopol, recalled in his book *The Black Sea Beneath Us*;

'Gen Ostryakov (Commander of the Black Sea Fleet Air Force) ordered that every available aircraft was shared by two or three pilots, and could therefore be used at the maximum possible rate of 12 to 15 sorties per 24-hour day. This required the groundcrew to work in two or three shifts to maintain the fighters in service. In addition, all the available I-16s and I-153s were to be equipped with the RO-82 rails for launching six RS-82 rocket projectiles in strikes on air and ground targets.'

Soon most of the naval fighters in-theatre were equipped with the six RS-82 launch rails. Denisov recalled one particular combat in which the rockets were used;

'In my earphones I heard my deputy, Capt Matveev, order "Attack the bombers with the RS simultaneously!" I saw G Matveev, V Borodin, N Nikolaev and N Sikov firing a salvo of 24 rocket projectiles. The group of eight Ju 88s immediately released their bombs over an unpopulated area and banked away. One burst into flames and went down into the sea by the mouth of the Northern Bay.'

Denisov began his air force career in 1936, initially flying TB-3 heavy bombers but later converting to fighters. At the outbreak of war he was serving with 8th IAP of the Black Sea Fleet Air Force, and during the first two months of the conflict Snr Lt Denisov was not able to distinguish himself. He had been detailed to form a new detached squadron, after

Snr Lt Vasiliy Matsievich poses with his I-16 during the Winter War. By June 1941 he was commanding 26th IAP, which was part of 7th IAK, Leningrad Anti-aircraft Defence. On the night of 25 October 1941 Matsievich shot down an He 111 bomber using RS-82 rocket projectiles. His wartime record included about 250 combat sorties and participation in 64 aerial combats, and he also shot down 24 enemy aircraft (16 individual and six shared with the I-16)

The 7.62 mm ShKAS machine guns of an I-16 Type 29 of 71st IAP are serviced and synchronised by armament technician I Belokon, while Sgt Segalaev checks the gunsight alignment from the cockpit. Note the RS-82 rocket projectiles, waiting to be test fired, beneath the fighter's wings. Having swapped its I-153s for I-16s in early 1942, 71st IAP flew myriad night defence missions over the Leningrad Front

An I-153 *Chayka* of the Black Sea Fleet Air Force patrols over Sebastopol Bay in late 1941

which he was ordered to ferry new Yak-1s from the Saratov factory to Black Sea Fleet air bases. However, it was while flying the trusty I-16 that Denisov achieved his first kills. On the night 30 August 1941, he and Lt Ruchkin were patrolling the approaches to Sebastopol when, by the light of the moon, they sighted a twin-engined Ju 88, which they shot down. The next day the remains of the bomber were fished out of the water and delivered to 8th IAP at Kacha-3 airfield. The following night Denisov took off alone and shot down an He 111 over the Northern Bay of Sebastopol.

A few months later he converted to the Yak-1 and was transferred to 7th IAP as a squadron CO. In October 1942 Denisov was promoted to command the regiment, before becoming CO of 11th GIAP, 62nd IAB of the Black Sea Fleet Air Force. By late 1945 Denisov was in the Far East, having claimed 13 individual and six shared kills in 536 combat sorties.

FINAL VICTORIES

One of the last Polikarpov-equipped fighter units in the frontline was 728th IAP of 256th IAD, which operated I-16s on the Kalinin Front in defence of Moscow from the start of the war through to March 1943, when it received Yak-7Bs. In the thick of the action throughout its time with the I-16, the regiment boasted a number of high-scoring aces, including Mikhail Baranov, Andrey Borovykh and Nikolay Ignatyev.

Many years after the war, in an interview between the latter pilot and aviation historian V Ivanov, Ignatyev confirmed that 728th IAP had flown early-production I-16 Type 5s in 1941-42 after most of the late-build examples had been lost in the first weeks of the war. The Type 5s had been pulled from training schools further east and sent to frontline units as attrition replacements. Despite the age of his mount, Ignatyev told Ivanov that he had felt neither fear nor inferiority when confronting enemy fighters. Moreover, he said that he and his comrades had always tried to act decisively and with daring. Most of them had arrived at the front with extensive experience of the I-16, having served as instructors.

With the Type 5 the ailerons, when lowered simultaneously, doubled as landing flaps. These ex-instructors discovered that lowering them by several degrees during normal flight improved stability to the extent that they could even let go of the control column! Having the ailerons lowered also improved economy and increased range.

When a group encountered the enemy, a pair of fighters would usually separate from the main formation to provide top cover. As Ignatyev put it, 'Whenever the Germans tried to avoid a dogfight, the detached pair would launch RS rockets to bring them back'.

As for the RS-82's effectiveness, Ignatyev had this to say;

'We moved from our base airfield at Selizharovo to a frontline airfield near Rzhev – the town itself had been captured by the Germans. In July 1942 our troops began an offensive to re-capture it. Six I-16s encountered

Featuring a non-standard camouflage scheme, this I-16 Type 10 of 728th IAP, Kalinin Front, was flown by several successful pilots including Khalkhin Gol veteran Arsenii Vorozheykin, Andrey Borovykh and Nikolay Ignatyev during the winter of 1942-43

An I-16 Type 17 piloted by Snr Lt Mikhail Vasilyev of 4th GIAP of the Baltic Fleet Air Force taxies in at Novaya Ladoga airfield after completing a mission during the spring of 1942. A participant in the fierce fighting over the Ladoga ports of Kobona and Lednyovo on 28 May 1942, Vasilyev claimed possibly as many as six individual and 20 shared victories with the I-16 prior to his death in action fighting Fw 190s over the Gulf of Finland on 5 May 1943

six groups of Ju 88s, nine in each group, escorted by 16 Me 109s. We approached them down-sun, and when our leader rocked his wings we simultaneously fired all 24 RS-82 projectiles. The result of that sudden salvo was that six Junkers went down and the rest of the formation broke up. We quickly engaged both the bombers and the fighters, downing three Me 109s without loss. The following day all six of us received the Order of Combat Red Banner from a member of the military council.'

Nikolay Ignatyev also received the title of Hero of the Soviet Union. By the end of the war he had achieved 26 individual and 15 shared kills during 412 combat sorties and 128 aerial engagements.

The I-16 pilot with the greatest combat experience of the RS-82 was Baltic Fleet pilot Vasiliy Golubev, who by early 1942 had been promoted to squadron CO within 4th GIAP. His most successful engagement with the rockets came on 12 March 1942 when, at 0500 hrs, 18 I-16s from the regiment took off to attack Mga railway station, near Lake Lodoga. The mission was being flown in support of an offensive launched that day by the Soviet 54th Army from the southern shore of the frozen lake.

'The strike force included two groups of six fighters from the 1st and 2nd Squadrons led by ace Mikhail Vasilyev', Golubev recalled. 'I should have led the covering group of six from the 3rd Squadron, but instead I instructed Alim Baysultanov to lead it. I didn't tell the CO. Before take-off, I told my wingman, Vladimir Dmitriev, to save at least half his ammunition for the return flight. I said I'd also do my best to use as little as possible during the attack by making mock passes. I didn't think the German fighters would allow us to return home unmolested after making a major attack on a strategic target like Mga railway station. I expected them to attack us over the frontline or as we approached our airfield.

'Having initially flown past the target in an effort to confuse enemy flak gunners, 18 I-16s approached Mga at minimal height and from a southerly direction so as to take the Germans by surprise. Two groups struck with rockets, cannon and machine guns from different directions. They targeted railway carriages crammed with troops and equipment, setting them on fire. Luckily there were no enemy fighters over the target, and we were able to make our second pass from three different directions, despite heavy anti-aircraft fire. According to reconnaissance reports, the resulting fires and explosions continued for hours after we left.

'Following our attack, Vasilyev wisely decided not to head straight home. Instead, he led the group over the Maluksinskiy swamp, before crossing the frontline into friendly territory. On our way we received a message from ground observers telling us about the large number of Messerschmitts waiting for us near our base. I'd anticipated that. Having failed to intercept us over the frontline, it was inevitable that the enemy would head for our airfield to pick off stragglers. Upon hearing this news I thought to myself now we shall see who outfoxes whom.

'I fell behind the main formation, flying 650 ft above the ground. Nine miles from home I saw flak shells exploding near the main formation, as well as close to the ground. That indicated that the Messerschmitts were nearby, roaming just above the forest. I accelerated and looked around – there they were! I spotted two Me 109Fs above the treetops. Vladimir Dmitriev had also spotted them and rocked his wings. I responded with a similar signal as I insisted on strict radio silence on such occasions.

'Our main formation was now starting to land, and I was still three miles from the airfield. Two enemy fighters stayed low and closed in on us – they had swallowed the bait. They thought we were easy meat, but wanted to show off by shooting us down over our own airfield. That was what I'd been waiting for. I accelerated and climbed. The "Messers'" exhausts belched smoke as their pilots put on boost as they approached for their attack.

'Having reached the middle of the airfield, I made a sharp maximum-g turn to the left to meet them face-to-face. Completing the turn at an altitude of 1000 ft, I saw the Me 109Fs. They weren't expecting such a rapid manoeuvre, and found themselves facing a head-on attack. Both "Messers" kept on approaching, their yellow noses pointing upwards. They probably couldn't believe that I had any ammunition left and thought I was just bluffing. The dark traces of their fire headed for my engine. I got the leader in my gunsight when he was 500 m away. Now I had just a second-and-a-half left – it was death or glory. The fingers of my right hand instinctively pressed the machine gun firing button. Three streaks of fire pierced the slender Messerschmitt's fuselage like some magic lightning strikes. Not waiting to see the outcome, I made a second sharp turn and saw the second "Messer" attempting to flee above and ahead of me. Instinctively, I pulled the firing handle, hardly bothering to assess the necessary deflection, and launched all four underwing RS-82 rockets in his direction. Four black clouds from the explosions appeared just behind the enemy's tail, but the "Messer" continued climbing steeply. I had no chance of catching him.

'Then, at about 5000 ft, he looped and dived, still shooting. What was up? Was he going to fight on by himself, or did he just want to make sure that it was his comrade's fighter that was lying smashed and blazing on the ground? No. He pulled out of his dive and began climbing again, before making another loop. Every second was priceless. By radio I ordered Dmitriev to attack him from below. I climbed rapidly to meet the German with my gunfire at the top of his third loop from a range of 50 m. But what was he up to? Then it struck me – he couldn't stop his fighter from continuously looping because his elevators had been jammed by fragments from my rockets. At the lowest point of his fourth loop the "Messer" hit the treetops and crash-landed on its belly, it wings torn off,

Vasiliy Golubev was one of the most successful aces of the Baltic Fleet Air Force, effectively using RS-82 rocket projectiles in combat. He claimed 39 individual and 12 shared victories, and 19 of the former were achieved in the I-16 while serving with 4th GIAP

right on the edge of the airfield. I saw the pilot jump out of the cockpit and limp towards my squadron's dispersal area. "Fritz" couldn't escape!

'I reported our success to the regimental command post, after which my wingman and I landed. The battle had been seen by the entire garrison, and both victories were greeted with loud cheers rolling across the airfield. Fifteen minutes later the groundcrews recovered the body of the second German pilot. Having escaped from his wrecked fighter he had died of wounds received during the battle.'

The latter was almost certainly 26-victory ace Unteroffizier Hans Schwartzkopf of 1./JG 54, although the identity of the first pilot remains a mystery. These successes took Vasiliy Golubev's score to 12 aircraft destroyed. He claimed two more kills over Lake Ladoga on 12 May, and he was rewarded with the title of Hero of the Soviet Union soon after.

While flying the I-16, Golubev would be credited with shooting down 19 enemy aircraft, including four Fw 190s, seven Bf 109s, four Ju 88s and two He 111s. At the end of 1943 he was given command of 4th GIAP. As one of the most successful Allied fighter pilots of World War 2, Golubev received many decorations, including the Order of the British Empire, but unlike many other senior commanders he continued to fly combat missions. On 13 January 1944 he shot down his 36th enemy aircraft, a Bf 110. Golubev's total score achieved during 589 sorties amounted to 39 individual and 12 shared victories. His military service continued after the war, and he went on to fly a number of jet aircraft.

Golubev was one of many pilots to prove the effectiveness of Polikarpov's fighters in combat, despite their age and clear obsolescence. The I-15 and I-16 had been advanced designs when they first entered production in the mid-1930s, subsequently proving their superiority over opposing fighters from Germany, Italy and Japan during various conflicts prior to World War 2. However, their combat careers continued far longer than they should have. Indeed, at the start of the Great Patriotic War in June 1941, the I-16 represented 40 per cent of the Soviet fighter inventory. But it soon became clear that even the latest versions were outclassed by the German fighters which now opposed them. Some units were still equipped with the stubby little fighter as late as mid-1943. Nevertheless, as this volume has revealed, in the hands of a skilled pilot, the I-16 could still be a deadly opponent almost a decade after its first appearance in Soviet ranks.

An I-16 Type 29 from an unidentified unit prepares to take off in early 1942. Its camouflage scheme has been applied in strict compliance with the 1941 marking directive, and it is armed with six RS-82 rockets

Lt Krichevskiy poses in a veteran, but noteworthy, I-16 Type 24 of 254th IAP at Budogoshch airfield, on the Leningrad Front, in 1943. The landing gear legs lack doors, one RS-82 rocket projectile has been installed under each wing and the wing-mounted ShKAS machine guns have non-standard extended barrels. The fighter displays five stars denoting five aerial victories and two tactical numbers, '1' on the rudder and '27' on the fuselage. The early-style red star on the tail is complemented by the newer version of the national marking, outlined in white, on the fuselage, and there is yet another red star on the propeller spinner. Also noteworthy is the radio aerial and the traces of an arrow which has been painted along the fuselage side, with its tip on the engine cowling

Deritend Engineering Services Ltd

21 Aldridge Road, Perry Barr,
Birmingham. B42 2TJ. England

Tel: +44 (0) 121 356 5545
Fax: +44 (0)121 356 8207
E-mail: sales@deritend.net
Website: www.deritend.net

Our ref: TB/JL/itinerary

25th June 2003

75 Westham House
Forth Drive
Chelmsley Wood
B37 6PT

For the attention of: Mr Tony Bassett

Hi Tony,

I trust you have had a safe and pleasant journey back from Karlia in Spain?

In speaking to Ray he has asked me to give an update on the service work we are kindly asking you and Ray to help with.

Spain

Pre GPW ASUs

APPENDICES

Soviet Polikarpov Aces

Surname	First Name	Rank (year)	Awards	Unit (operating I-15/I-153/I-16) or campaign	Number of victories (individual + shared)
Abramov	Vladimir	Capt (1943)	HSU/OL/OCRB	71st IAP, 10th GIAP	10+15 (total 29)
Abramov	Petr	Capt (1941)	-	195th IAP	5+10 in I-16
Adonkin	Aleksander	Capt (1944)	HSU/OL/three OCRB	72nd SAP, 78th IAP, 27th IAP	17+4 (5 in I-153 and I-16)
Agureev	Aleksander	Capt (1942)	OCRB	5th IAP, 4th GIAP	7+2
Antonenko	Aleksey	Capt (1941)	HSU	13th IAP	4+6
Baranov	Mikhail	Maj (1945)	HSU	728th IAP, 157th IAP	20+9 (9+3 in I-16)
Baturin	Aleksander	Maj (1943)	HSU	71st IAP	18+12 (9+1 in I-153)
Batyaev	Vasiliy	Capt (1945)	HSU	88th IAP, 53rd GIAP	9+11 (5+8 in I-16)
Bedukadze	Shakro	Snr Lt (1943)	OCRB	11th IAP, 4th GIAP	11+3 (9+2 in I-16)
Blagoveshchenskiy	Aleksey	Col (1938)	HSU	China	7+16
Bobrov	Vladimir	Jnr Lt (1938)	HSU	Spain, GPW	43+20
Borovykh	Andrey	Maj (1945)	HSU twice	728th IAP	32+14 (8+9 in I-16)
Brinko	Petr	Snr Lt (1941)	HSU	13th IAP	15+2 and balloon in I-16
Bulaev	Aleksander	Maj (1942)	HSU	158th IAP, 159th IAP	17+5 (2+3 in Winter War in I-16)
Chernykh	Sergey	Lt (1937)	HSU	Spain	5+2 in I-16
Chizhyk	Fedor	Snr Lt (1942)	-	265th IAP	6+3 in I-16
Danilov	Andrey	Snr Lt (1941)	-	127th IAP	9
Danilov	Stepan	Maj (1939)	HSU	56th IAP Khalkhin Gol	8 in I-16
Denisov	Konstantin	Capt (1941)	HSU	8th IAP	13+6
Dodonov	Semen	Snr Lt (1943)	-	40th IAP	6+11 in I-16
Eremenko	Ivan	Capt (1938)	HSU	Spain	9 in I-15
Fedoseev	Mikhail	Lt (1938)	HSU	Spain, GPW	25 (5 in I-16 in Spain)
Fomin	Efim	Snr Lt (1941)	-	147th IAP	5 in I-153
Galchenko	Leonid	Capt (1942)	HSU/OL/OCRB twice	145th IAP, 609th IAP	24+12 (7 in I-16)
Garanin	Vladimir	Capt (1945)	HSU	88th IAP, 254th IAP	11+1 (5+1 in I-16)
Golubev	Vasiliy	Capt (1943)	HSU/OL twice/seven OCRB	4th GIAP	39+12 (19 in I-16)
Grachev	Ivan	Maj (1944)	HSU	26th IAP, 191st IAP	13+4 (7+4 in I-16)
Gritsevets	Sergey	Maj (1939)	HSU twice	Spain, Khalkhin Gol	19+?
Gubenko	Anton	Snr Lt (1938)	HSU	China	7
Ignatyev	Nikolay	Snr Lt (1943)	HSU	728th IAP	26+15
Kalabushkin	Ivan	Maj (1945)	HSU	123rd IAP	6 on I-153 (total 6+6)
Kardanov	Kubati	Capt (1943)	HSU	88th IAP	7+12 (8 in I-16)
Kharitonov	Vasiliy	Maj (1944)	HSU	195th IAP, 26th IAP	6+10 in I-16 (total 18+16)
Kokkinaki	Konstantin	Lt (1938)	HSU	China, GPW	10+4 (7 in I-16)
Kovalenko	Aleksander	Maj (1942)	HSU	72nd SAP	7+1 in I-16 (total 11+1)
Kozachenko	Petr	Col (1945)	HSU	China, GPW	27+8
Kozhanov	Petr	Capt (1943)	HSU	13th IAP, 4th GIAP	6+3 in I-16 (total 9+4)
Krasnoyurchenko	Ivan	Lt (1939)	HSU	22nd IAP Khalkhin Gol	8+16 (5 in I-16)
Kravchenko	Grigoriy	Lt Gen (1943)	HSU twice	China, Khalkhin Gol (22nd IAP), GPW (11th IAD)	7+4 in I-16 (and 4? in La-5)
Kudymov	Dmitriy	Capt (1941)	five OCRB	China, 9th IAP, 7th IAP, 13th OIAE (GPW)	4 in China, 8+29 in World War 2
Kuznetsov	Anatoliy	Lt (1942)	HSU	13th IAP, 4th GIAP	5+6 in I-16
Lakeev	Ivan	Maj (1939)	HSU/four OCRB	Spain, Khalkin Gol, GPW	16+20 in I-16
Lazarev	Mikhail	Lt (1941)	-	191st IAP	6+1 in I-16
Lomakin	Anatoliy	Snr Lt (1943)	HSU/OL twice/OCRB twice	21st IAP	7+22 (6+? in I-16)

Matsievich	Vasiliy	Snr Lt (1941)	HSU	26th IAP of 7th IAK	24 (16+6 as of June 1942)
Milodan	Andrey	Capt (1941)	-	131st IAP	5+2 in I-16
Mironov	Viktor	Snr Lt (1941)	OCRB	145th IAP	10+15 (5? in I-16)
Moklyak	Alexandr	Lt (1941)		67th IAP	5 in I-16
Moskalchuk	Vasiliy	Capt (1942)	OCRB	249th IAP, 88th IAP	9+2 in I-16 and I-153
Muraviitskiy	Luka	Snr Lt (1941)	OL	29th IAP, 127th IAP	12+35 in I-16
Neustruev	Ivan	Lt Col (1945)	HSU	195th IAP, 26th IAP	5+6 in I-16 (total 15+10)
Nikhamin	David	Lt Col (1945)	OL	32nd IAP, 101st OIAE	5+2 in I-16 (total 9+3)
Noga	Mitrofan	Snr Lt (1939)	HSU	70th IAP Khalkhin Gol	27+3 (9+2 in I-16)
Novikov	Egor	Jnr Lt (1941)	HSU	191st IAP	9+4 in I-16
Obiralov	Viktor	Capt (1943)	-	286th IAP	9+1 in I-16 (total 15+1)
Oskalenko	Dmitriy	Capt (1942)	HSU	193rd IAP, 194th IAP	12+3 in I-16
Petrov	Petr	Maj (1943)	HSU	68th IAP, 254th IAP	10 in I-15bis and I-16
Pidtykan	Ivan	Snr Lt (1942)	HSU	195th IAP, 26th IAP, 123rd IAP	12+10 in I-16
Plavskiy	Vladimir	Snr Lt (1942)	-	191st IAP, 127th IAP	8+2 in I-16
Pokrovskiy	Vladimir	Capt (1943)	HSU	72nd SAP	4+2 in I-153 (total 12+6)
Pokryshev	Petr	Snr Lt (1941)	HSU twice/OL/three OCRB	7th IAP, 154th IAP, 159th IAP	11+7 in 1-16 (total 38 +8)
Putyakov	Sergey	Capt (1942)	-	29th IAP, 127th IAP	5 in I-16 and I-153
Ragozin	Yakov	Snr Lt (1941)	-	67th IAP	5 in I-16
Rakhov	Viktor	Snr Lt (1939)	HSU	22nd IAP Khalkhin Gol	8+6 in I-16
Rychagov	Pavel	Snr Lt (1937)	HSU/OL twice/three OCRB	Spain	6+14 in I-15
Safonov	Boris	Lt Col (1942)	HSU twice	72nd SAP (2nd GIAP)	20+6 (17 or 14 in I-16)
Samonov	Nikolay	Lt (1942)	-	436th IAP, 176th IAP	7+1 in I-16 (total 9+4)
Savchenko	Aleksander	Capt (1944)	HSU	191st IAP, 127th IAP	4+4 in I-16 (total 15+16)
Semenenko	Petr	Sgt Maj (1941)	-	72nd SAP	6+1 in I-16
Serbin	Ivan	Deputy Commander for Political Education (1941)		61st IAB	5+3 in I-16 and I-153
Serov	Anatoliy	Snr Lt (1938)	HSU/OL/OCRB twice	Spain	8 in I-15
Shestakov	Lev	Col (1944)	HSU	Spain, 69th IAP, 19th IAP	23+44 (5+8 in I-16)
Shmelkov	Nikolay	Snr Lt (1937)	HSU/OL/ORB	Spain, 145th IAP	5 in I-15 in Spain (total 18)
Shytov	Aleksander	Snr Lt (1942)	-	12th OIAE, 71st IAP	8+1 in I-153
Skobarikhin	Vitt	Snr Lt (1939)	HSU	22nd IAP Khalkhin Gol	5+6 in I-16
Slivka	Semen	Snr Lt (1942)	-	88th IAP	5+1 in I-16
Smirnov	Boris	Snr Lt (1938)	HSU	Spain, Khalkhin Gol	6 in I-16
Smirnov	Viktor	Sgt Maj (1942)	OCRB twice	629th IAP	7+2 in I-16
Solovyev	Konstantin	Maj (1943)	HSU	71st, 13th IAP	4+8 in I-153
Sorokin	Zakhar	Snr Lt (1941)	HSU/OL	72nd SAP (2nd GIAP)	5 in I-16 (total 18)
Stepanov	Evgeniy	Capt (1939)	HSU	Spain, 22nd IAP Khalkhin Gol	10 in Spain and 3 in Mongolia
Talalikhin	Viktor	Snr Lt (1941)	HSU/OL	177th IAP	3 in Winter War and 4 in World War 2
Tatarchuk	Aleksey	Maj (1944)	-	286th IAP	6+1 in I-16 (total 7+1)
Terekhin	Nikolay	Snr Lt (1941)	OL	161st IAP	17 in I-16
Trubachenko	Vasiliy	Capt (1939)	HSU	70th IAP Khalkhin Gol	8 in I-16
Tsokolaev	Gennadiy	Snr Lt (1942)	HSU/OL twice/OCRB twice	4th GIAP	7+15
Tsyganov	Evgeniy	Capt (1943)	HSU	5th IAP, 13th IAP, 4th GIAP	10+2 in I-16 (total 11+7)
Vasilyev	Mikhail	Capt (1943)	HSU	4th GIAP	6+16 in I-16
Vorozheykin	Arseniy	Snr Lt (1941)	HSU twice	22nd IAP Khalkhin Gol, GPW	6+12 in Khalkhin Gol, 45 in 1941-45
Zakharov	Georgiy	Maj Gen (1941)	HSU	Spain, China, GPW	18+4
Zaytsev	Aleksander	Capt (1939)	HSU	70th IAP Khalkhin Gol	8 in Spain, 6 in Khalkhin Gol and 1 in 1944-45
Zherdev	Nikolay	Capt (1939)	HSU	70th IAP Khalkhin Gol	16+6 in I-16
Zhuykov	Grigoriy	Maj (1944)	OL/OCRB	191st IAP	7 in I-16

HSU – Hero of the Soviet Union

OL – Order of Lenin

OCRB – Order of Combat Red Banner

GPW – Great Patriotic War

IAP – Fighter Aviation Regiment

GIAP – Guards Fighter Aviation Regiment

SAP – Combined Aviation Regiment

IAD – Fighter Aviation Division

IAB – Fighter Aviation Brigade

OIAE – Independent Fighter Aviation Squadron

Colour Plates

1

I-15 of Ivan Pavlov, Commander of the Moscow Military District Aviation, 1934-35

This aircraft features an unusually high-quality finish in which the duralumin skin of the forward fuselage has been polished in a method known as 'freeze'. The fuselage displays a red banner with the legend *For VKP(b)* ('For the All-Russian Communist Party of Bolsheviks'), while a bent white arrow was applied to the red-painted rudder. Fokker D.XIII, I-4 and I-5 fighters flown by Pavlov between 1927 and 1931 were also known to have featured a similar colour scheme. A veteran fighter pilot of World War 1, he formed the 1st Soviet Air Group in 1918 and headed Red Army aviation on the Southern Front from September 1920. Over the next ten years Pavlov held a number of senior command positions in the Red Army Air Force, and was Commander of the Moscow Military District Aviation in 1934-35. Pavlov died in 1936, however.

2

I-15 of an unidentified VVS RKKA fighter regiment during the mid-1930s

This aircraft displays the standard VVS RKKA camouflage of the period. The red star has a thin black outline and a black circle within it, this style of national marking first appearing on aircraft built at the Duks factory in Moscow in the 1920s. It continued to be sporadically applied to batches of Polikarpov fighters built at the facility into the 1940s. Although this marking style is known to have been painted onto aircraft from other factories as well, no documentation has yet been found officially approving its application. During the air battles fought in the Khalkhin Gol conflict, Soviet pilots sometimes misinterpreted the black circle in the star for the Japanese Hinomaru national marking, so its use was subsequently discontinued.

3

I-15 probably flown by Mikhail Yakushin, 1a/*Gruppo* 26, Alcalá de Henares, Spain, July 1937

This aircraft was assigned to 1a/*Gruppo* 26, which was the I-15 volunteer group commanded by Ivan Eremenko in 1937 during the Spanish Civil War. It is believed that Mikhail Yakushin was flying the I-15 on the night of 27 July 1937 when he shot down a Ju-52/3m of the *Legion Condor*. Built by Factory No 1 in Moscow, this aircraft does not display the standard tactical number (prefixed by CA- for Spanish-built machines or CC- for those supplied from the USSR) typically worn by I-15s in Spain. It should be noted that all I-15s delivered to the Spanish Republican Air Force had already seen service in the VVS RKKA, arriving in-theatre with their red stars painted out.

4

I-15 of Evgeny Antonov, 1a/*Gruppo* 26, Bajaralos, Spain, December 1937

This fighter, which displays a white zero in a circle on its rudder, also lacks CA- or CC- tactical numbers. It was routinely flown by Evgeny Antonov, squadron commander of la *Escuadrilla* of *Gruppo* 26. Antonov fought in Spain from 31 May 1937 until 28 January 1938, and during this time he initially commanded a flight and later a squadron. He logged about 210 flying hours in Spain and shot down two enemy aircraft. Although he is not listed as an ace, Antonov was senior enough to be allocated his own I-15, and this is confirmed by a photograph showing him with his 'personal' aircraft (see page 24). After his return from Spain, Antonov flew as a member of the 'Red Fives' aerobatic group and then saw further combat against Finland in the Winter War. He was killed in 1942 when the Yak-1 that he was flight-testing crashed.

5

I-15 of 4a/*Gruppo* 26, Valencia, Spain, January 1938

This Polikarpov biplane fighter displays the tactical number CA-018, the CA- prefix denoting that it had been built in Spain, while the three digits indicate that the aircraft was just the 18th locally-constructed I-15 to go into service with the Republican Air Force.

6

I-15bis of the Kuomintang Chinese Air Force, Nanchang, China, 1938

This aircraft displays the standard camouflage and markings of Kuomintang China during the conflict with Japan. Such

91

fighters were usually flown by Soviet volunteer pilots, and specific personal or unit markings were not generally applied to them. However, ace Georgiy Zakharov recalls that the fuselage of the fighter flown by his commanding officer displayed a large zero for ease of identification in the air. There is no photographic confirmation of the shape and position of the marking.

7

I-15bis of the Kuomintang Chinese Air Force, Nanchang, China, 1938

This I-15bis also featured the serial number 305 on its fin, in addition to the standard camouflage and markings of the period. No fewer than 347 I-15s and I-15bis were supplied to the CAF by the USSR between October 1937 and September 1939.

8

I-15bis of Snr Lt Vladimir Abramov, 71st IAP, Baltic Fleet Air Force, Leningrad Front, USSR, summer 1941

This fighter, together with an I-153 displaying the tactical number '42', was flown by Vladimir Abramov. Unofficial sources state that he used this aircraft, and his I-153, to score at least five aerial victories. Altogether Abramov flew about 600 combat sorties, participated in 67 aerial engagements and officially scored ten individual and 15 shared victories. However, some sources claim that his overall tally was as high as 29 kills.

9

I-153 of 22nd IAP, 1st Army Group Air Force, Tamsag Bulag, Mongolia, early summer 1939

Finished in overall aluminium, this aircraft wears the standard scheme applied to fighters arriving in Mongolia in the summer of 1939 for operations in the Soviet-Japanese conflict over the Khalkhin Gol River. By 20 August the three air regiments of the 1st Army Group Air Force had 67 examples of the then new I-153 on strength out of a total of 70 that were eventually deployed to the area. Combat losses for the period from 28 July to 15 September 1939 amounted to 16 I-153s, with six more written off in accidents. Despite this heavy rate of attrition, the I-153 was a match for the JAAF's Ki-27.

10

I-153 of Vladimir Kalachev, 22nd IAP, 1st Army Group Air Force, Tamsag Bulag, Mongolia, August 1939

Built by Factory No 1 in July 1939, this fighter would have originally been delivered in an overall aluminium paint scheme as seen in the previous profile. However, soon after their arrival in Mongolia all the I-153s assigned to 22nd IAP received an improvised camouflage scheme of either green dots or stripes, as seen here, applied over the silver to make the aircraft less visible from the air. Kalachev was the regiment's commissar, and he claimed two victories in Mongolia. He later 'made ace' flying MiG-3s in World War 2, but was killed in action on 28 June 1942 while serving as CO of 15th IAP. The I-153 flown by 70th IAP's CO, and high-scoring ace, Sergey Gritsevets, was similarly camouflaged. According to some sources, Gritsevets claimed as many as 12 victories while flying I-16s and I-153s during the Khalkhin Gol conflict.

11

I-153 of Lt Sergey Zhukovskiy, 127th IAP, Western Military District, Leningrad Front, USSR, summer 1941

Painted in an overall aluminium finish, this aircraft was flown nine times by Lt Zhukovskiy, a squadron commander with 127th IAP, on 22 June 1941. He used it to claim one individual and three shared victories on this date, and he would subsequently see considerable action flying La-5 fighters with 13th IAP and 41 and 88 GIAPs. Zhukovskiy survived the war with 13 individual and 15 shared victories to his name.

12

I-153 of Snr Lt Aleksander Adonkin, 72nd SAP, Northern Fleet Air Force, Vaenga, USSR, summer 1941

This aircraft features a standard green/light blue camouflage scheme, with its fin and rudder painted white. The fighter also has the Duks factory national insignia applied. Snr Lt Aleksander Adonkin was one of several successful pilots from the unit to fly this aircraft, although it is unclear whether he claimed any victories with it. Adonkin was credited with five kills in the I-153 and I-16 in an overall total of 17 individual and four shared victories – the bulk of his successes came flying Hurricanes with 78th IAP and 2nd GIAP. Having flown 365 sorties and fought 42 aerial combats, Adonkin lost his life on 17 March 1944 when his P-39 was shot down over the Finnish island of Eckerö.

13

I-153 of Snr Lt Aleksander Baturin, 71st IAP, Baltic Fleet Air Force, Bychye Pole, USSR, summer 1942

This aircraft is painted in a standard camouflage scheme comprising green/black uppersurfaces with light blue undersides. Its pilot, Snr Lt Baturin, had been seriously wounded and almost blinded in one eye at the end of August 1941. He was, however, able to remain on active service through to war's end, by which time his victory tally had reached 18 individual and 12 shared. Half of Baturin's individual kills were claimed in the I-153, with his most successful period in the fighter coming on 3-4 April 1942 when he was credited with four and one shared victories – the latter was a Finnish Fokker D.XXI from LLv 30, although the Finns denied losing any aircraft on this date.

14

I-153 of Capt Petr Biskup, 71st IAP, Baltic Fleet Air Force, Bychye Pole, USSR, summer 1942

This long-lived fighter saw intensive combat during 1941-42, being flown by No 1 Squadron CO Capt Petr Biskup among other pilots. By the end of the war Biskup had shot down five enemy aircraft and shared in the destruction of another five. At least two of these victories were achieved while he was at the controls of an I-153.

15

I-16 Type 5 of 5 *Escuadrilla/Grupo de Caza*, Spain, late 1937

This fighter's standard camouflage scheme was applied at Factory No 21 at Nizhniy Novgorod, although the engine cowling and spinner were probably painted black during its service in the Soviet Union – many of the I-16s supplied to the Republicans had seen prior service with the VVS RKKA. Once handed over to the Spanish, the fighters were adorned with red identification stripes on their wings and fuselages and the Republican three-colour marking on the rudder. Note that the Type 5 version of the I-16 was fitted with a sliding cockpit canopy, which is seen here in the open position. This fighter may well have been flown by Soviet pilots prior its capture when Nationalist forces overran its unidentified base at the end of 1937.

16

I-16 Type 5 of 5 *Escuadrilla/Grupo de Caza*, Spain, summer 1937

This early-build Type 5 also boasts a sliding canopy, although it is depicted here in the closed position. As with the aircraft in the previous profile, the fighter displays the standard ex-VVS RKKA green/light blue camouflage scheme with Republican air force markings.

17

I-16 Type 5 of 5 *Escuadrilla/Grupo de Caza*, Cartagena, Spain, summer 1937

This fighter was flown by Soviet volunteer pilots charged with providing air cover for the Spanish city of Cartagena in mid-1937. Note the non-standard application of its individual identification number on the fin in white, rather than on the rudder in black.

18

I-16 Type 10 of Grigoriy Kravchenko, Kuomintang Chinese Air Force, Hankou, China, April 1938

This aircraft appears in the standard green camouflage scheme worn by all I-16s to see service with the CAF. The tactical number and Kuomintang markings were applied soon after the fighter had been delivered to China. 'White 70' was flown on a number of occasions by ranking Soviet ace in China Grigoriy Kravchenko during the spring and summer of 1938.

19

I-16 Type 10 fighter of the Kuomintang Chinese Air Force, Hankou, China, summer 1938

I-16s adorned with large tactical numbers on their fuselages were typically flown by Soviet pilots during the conflict with Japan. A variety of spinner colours were also worn by Polikarpov fighters in China, although their significance remains unknown. In the USSR, pilots sent on such combat 'visits' were usually considered to be 'volunteers' drawn directly from frontline VVS RKKA regiments. Upon returning home they were regarded as heroes by both their comrades and the civilian population alike.

20

I-16 Type 10 of 70th IAP, 1st Combat Air Group, Tamsag Bulag, Mongolia, May 1939

This fighter is seen in the aluminium scheme that adorned all VVS RKKA Polikarpov fighters in Mongolia at the start of the Khalkhin Gol conflict in May 1939. 'Black 7' was one of just 24 I-16s assigned to 70th IAP when the border dispute erupted into undeclared war with Japan. Many more were rushed to Mongolia within weeks of the conflict commencing.

21

I-16 Type 10 of Snr Lt Viktor Rakhov, 22nd IAP, 1st Combat Air Group, Tamsag Bulag, Mongolia, summer 1939

Replacement I-16s hastily sent to Mongolia with 22nd IAP arrived in the standard VVS RKKA green/light blue camouflage scheme, which also included a red tip to the fin. The only marking that was unique to the regiment's fighters was the horizontal white stripe on the fin. This aircraft was routinely flown by Snr Lt Viktor Rakhov, who claimed eight individual and six shared victories (many in this machine) during his time in Mongolia.

22

I-16 Type 10 of 22nd IAP, 1st Combat Air Group, Tamsag Bulag, Mongolia, July-August 1939

An attrition replacement aircraft despatched to Mongolia at the height of the conflict over the Khalkhin Gol River, this I-16 has had its fuselage identification markings painted out and a non-standard silver stripe applied around the rear fuselage. The latter was seen on a number of aircraft flown by 22nd IAP in July 1939, it being assumed that the stripe was applied to enable other Soviet aircraft to quickly identify I-16s from the regiment in the heat of battle.

23

I-16 Type 10 of Snr Lt Vitt Skobarikhin, 22nd IAP, 1st Combat Air Group, Tamsag Bulag, Mongolia, summer 1939

Painted in the standard green/light blue camouflage scheme, this aircraft also has a red star applied to its propeller spinner. Its pilot, Snr Lt Vitt Skobarikhin, was a squadron commander in 22nd IAP who participated in aerial combat in Mongolia from 27 May until the conflict ended on 16 September. By then he had flown 169 combat sorties and fought in 26 aerial battles, during which he shot down five Japanese aircraft and shared in the destruction of six more. On 20 July, while flying this I-16, Skobarikhin had performed a successful ramming attack on a Ki-27 fighter, after which he landed the aircraft safely at Tamsag Bulag.

24

I-16 Type 10 of Snr Lt Leonid Galchenko, 145th IAP, Vaenga, USSR, summer 1941

This aircraft features the standard green/light blue camouflage scheme, with a white propeller spinner. The white band on the fuselage was probably applied after the I-16 had been repaired following combat damage. A squadron commander with 145th IAP, Galchenko shot down seven enemy aircraft in three months during the bitter defence of the Polar harbours of Murmansk and Arkhangelsk.

25

I-16 Type 10 of Snr Lt Nikolay Ignatyev, 728th IAP, Kalinin Front, USSR, winter 1942-43

Featuring a mixed, non-standard, camouflage scheme, this aircraft was flown by several successful pilots during the winter of 1942-43, including Khalkhin Gol veteran Arsenii Vorozheykin, Andrey Borovykh and Nikolay Ignatyev. All three pilots would 'make ace' with 728th IAP, either flying the I-16 or its Yak-7B replacement.

26
I-16 Type 10 of Maj Gen Ivan Lakeev, 235th IAD, Kuban Front, USSR, late 1941

The standard camouflage scheme applied to this aircraft is combined with a red-painted front to the engine cowling, as well as a red spinner and lower rudder section. The port side of the fuselage bears the inscriptions *For VKPb!* ('All-Russian Communist Party of Bolsheviks!') and *named after Lenin*. Lakeev fought in the Spanish Civil War, arriving in Spain in the autumn of 1936 as a lieutenant to fly I-16s. Promoted to squadron commander in May 1937, he had been credited with two individual and three shared victories by the end of his tour. After his return to the USSR, Lakeev was promoted to the rank of major and awarded the title of Hero of the Soviet Union. Having subsequently fought in the Khalkhin Gol conflict, where he claimed one more victory, Lakeev was made commander of 235th IAD in the summer of 1941. Although he frequently led the unit into combat (his mission tally in three wars exceeded 500), he failed to add any claims to his impressive pre-war tally of 16 individual and 20 shared victories.

27
I-16 Type 17 of Snr Lt Arseniy Vorozheykin, 22nd IAP, 1st Combat Air Group, Tamsag Bulag, Mongolia, August 1939

Armed with two 20 mm cannon, this aircraft was flown by Arseniy Vorozheykin, commissar of the 5th Squadron, from late July through to mid-September 1939. During the Soviet-Japanese conflict in Mongolia, Vorozheykin flew more than 160 combat sorties and fought in 30 aerial battles, during which he was credited with six individual and twelve shared victories. He would also enjoy considerable success in World War 2.

28
I-16 Type 17 of Snr Lt Mikhail Vasilyev, 4th GIAP, Baltic Fleet Air Force, Novaya Ladoga, USSR, spring 1942

Vasilyev flew a total of 440 combat sorties, during which he shot down four (or six) enemy aircraft and shared in the destruction of no fewer than 20 more. He had reached the rank of captain, and was also a Hero of the Soviet Union, when on 5 May 1943, as a squadron commander, Vasilyev was shot down and killed while dogfighting with Fw 190s over the Gulf of Finland near Leningrad.

29
I-16 Type 24 of Snr Lt Nikolay Terekhin, 161st IAP, Belorussian Front, USSR, summer 1941

A squadron commander with 161st IAP in June 1941, Terekhin was an ace who flew 250 combat sorties and scored a total of 17 victories. On 10 July 1941, while flying this I-16, he shot down a Ju 88 over Mogilev and destroyed another bomber by ramming it. Indeed, three of Terekhin's first six victories were achieved via *Taran* attacks.

30A and 30B
I-16 Type of Snt Lt Vasiliy Golubev, 7th IAP, Leningrad Front, USSR, summer 1941

This aircraft has had its standard green camouflage scheme partially painted over with black paint to make the fighter less conspicuous when viewed from above – VVS RKKA aircraft tended to be flown at considerably lower altitudes than their Luftwaffe counterparts. This modification was officially introduced just days prior to the German invasion on 22 June 1941. Aside from the camouflage modification, the application of national markings also changed so that red stars were applied to the underside of the left wing, fuselage sides and tailfin only. This particular machine also bore the tactical number '13', which was actually considered to be lucky by some Soviet fighter pilots. Baltic ace Vasiliy Golubev was not one of them, however, and he soon had the number changed to 33.

31
I-16 Type 24 Snr Lt Anatoliy Lomakin, 21st IAP, Baltic Sea Air Force, Leningrad Front, USSR, 1942-43

The non-standard shape of the red star on this aircraft's vertical tail is noteworthy. Snr Lt Lomakin was a late starter with the I-16, having been posted to 21st IAP in March 1942 after completing his flying training. Flying in defence of Leningrad, he found himself in the thick of the action. Lomakin's most notable success came almost a year later on 23 February 1943 when he claimed two Fw 190s destroyed with RS-82 rockets. His regiment finally began to receive Yak-1s shortly after this clash, although Lomakin continued to fly the I-16 well into the summer of that year. By September 1943 he had completed 452 sorties and claimed seven victories during 49 aerial engagements. Made a Hero of the Soviet Union on 21 January 1944, Lomakin was shot down and killed just four days later. By then his tally stood at seven individual and 22 shared victories.

32
I-16 Type 24 of Snr Lt Gennadiy Tsokolaev, 4th GIAP, Baltic Fleet Air Force, Leningrad Front, USSR, February 1942

Unusually for the period, this fighter had light grey upper surfaces. Note also the Guards emblem on the starboard side of the fuselage. The aircraft was routinely flown by Hero of Soviet Union Snr Lt Tsokolaev, who was both a veteran of the Winter War and an I-16 ace.

33
I-16 Type 24 of Lt Krichevskiy, 254th IAP, Budogoshch, near Leningrad, USSR, 1943

The five stars painted just behind the cockpit on this machine represent a rare case of a personal scoreboard being applied to a Polikarpov fighter. Such markings became commonplace on Soviet fighters from late 1942 onwards, but were not often seen on I-153s or I-16s. The unusual appearance of this aircraft – mixed versions of the national marking, non-standard numbering and a victory tally – has been confirmed by photographic evidence (see page 88), although no further information about its assigned pilot, Lt Krichevskiy, or his victories, has so far come to light.

34
I-16 Type 24 of Sgt Grigoriy Guryanov, 4th GIAP, Baltic Fleet Air Force, Leningrad Front, USSR, spring 1942

A temporary white winter camouflage scheme using lime-based paint has been applied to this aircraft, which was flown by Sgt (later Snr Lt) Grigoriy Guryanov. Prior to switching to the vastly superior La-5 in 1943, he scored four individual and three shared victories with the I-16 out of a total of seven individual and three shared kills. Guryanov perished on 25 August 1944 when his fighter was brought down by anti-aircraft artillery.

35
I-16 Type 24 of 13th OIAE, Baltic Fleet Air Force, Nizino, USSR, summer 1940

This aircraft displays the standard green/light blue camouflage finish seen on all VVS RKKA fighters pre-June 1941, but the markings on its tail could possibly identify it as being the mount of a unit commander.

36A and 36B
I-16 Type 24 of Snr Lt Boris Safonov, 72nd SAP, Northern Fleet Air Force, Vaenga, USSR, summer 1941

It is likely that this aircraft, which displays the patriotic slogan *For Stalin!* on the port side of its fuselage, was flown by squadron commander Snr Lt Boris Safonov. Although he is known to have flown other Polikarpov fighters during his service with the regiment, there is a photograph (see page 75) showing the famous ace standing near this particular fighter, which also featured the legend *For Communism!* on the starboard side.

37
I-16 Type 24 of Snr Sgt S Surjenko, 72nd SAP, Northern Fleet Air Force, Vaenga, USSR, summer 1941

This aircraft was another of 72nd SAP's I-16s to be hastily adorned with a patriotic slogan (in this case *For the USSR!*) in the immediate wake of the German invasion of the Soviet Union. Its pilot was Snr Sgt S Surjenko, who was photographed in the cockpit of the fighter at the same time that Boris Safonov was seen near the I-16 featured in the previous profile

38
I-16 Type 29 of Snr Lt Petr Brinko, 13th IAP, Baltic Fleet Air Force, Leningrad Front, USSR, summer 1941

This fighter displays the standard green/light blue camouflage scheme, together with a red tip to the fin. Its pilot, Snr Lt Petr Brinko, was a veteran of both the Khalkhin Gol conflict and the Winter War. Credited with 15 individual and two shared victories in the first three months of the Great Patriotic War, he became one of the first two naval pilots to be made a Hero of the Soviet Union on 14 July 1941. Brinko was killed by flak shortly after destroying an observation balloon on 14 September 1941.

Back cover
I-16 Type 29 of Snr Lt Vasiliy Golubev, 13th IAP, Baltic Fleet Air Force, Novaya Ladoga, USSR, late 1941

High-scoring ace Snr Lt Golubev shot down five enemy aircraft while flying this fighter in the defence of Hanko naval base. One of the USSR's most successful Polikarpov pilots, he was credited with shooting down 19 enemy aircraft with the I-16, including four Fw 190s, seven Bf 109s, four Ju 88s and two He 111s. Golubev's unit was redesignated 4th GIAP on 18 January 1942.

INDEX

References to illustrations are shown in **bold**. Plates are shown with page and caption locators in brackets.

SPANISH CIVIL WAR 1936-9

HEROES OF THE SOVIET UNION HSUs

34 AIRCREW (PILOTS, NAVIGATORS, GUNNERS)

31/12/36 16 HSUs AWARDED 11 TO AVIATORS
INCLUDING ONE ITALIAN AIRMAN
PRIMO GIBELLI KIA 13/11/36
ON THE MADRID FRONT.

31/12/36

1 KARP KOVTUN
2. PAVEL RYCHAGOV
3. NIKOLAY SHMELKOV
4. BORIS TIRZHANSKY
5. SERGEY CHERNYKH
6.
7.
8.
9.
10.
11 PRIMO GIBELLI
12
13
14
15
16

media

Mr Neil Bassett
Flat 75
Westham House
Forth Drive
B37 6PT

November 2012

DML24588/T11/BM038390601   B360986

The price of your Virgin Media services is going up. But you're still getting great value for money.

Dear Mr Bassett,

We wanted to let you know that, from 1st February 2013,* the price of your Virgin Media services will increase by £5.34 a month. It's never nice when prices go up but it means we can continue to give you the best home entertainment and services.

HSU Spanish Civil War.

KARP KOVTUN   1-15 ⒷKIA 31/12/36   13/11/3?

PAVEL RYCHAGOV   1-15 31/12/36

NIKOLAY SCHMELKOV   1-15 31/12/36

BORIS TURZHANSKIY   1-15 31/12/36

IVAN KOPETS   #1-15 21/6/37   + Foreig Tur?

PETR PUMPUR   1-15/1-16 4/7/37

IVAN EREMENKO   1-15 28/10/37

ANATOLIY SEROV   1-15   2/3/38

ALEKSANDER OSIPENKO 1-15 22/2/39

E   STEPANOV

E   ERLYKIN

A   OSADCHIY

G   ZAKHAROV

V   KONDRAT

SERGEY CHERNYKH 1-16 31/12/36

    DENISOV 1-16   4/4/37

KONSTANTIN KOLESNIKOV 4/7/37   KIFA 12/5/3?

BORIS SMIRNOV 1-16 Span/RGG 17/11/39

SERGEY GRITSEVETS 1-16 22/2/39 29/8/3?

MIKHIL FEDOSEEV   KIA 23/3/42 Ⓟ HSU

VLADIMIR BOBROV   HSU 1991

future, for you and your family.

And now that the maximum discount on the purchase price of your home under Right to Buy has been raised to £75,000, it could be more affordable for you.

Of course, buying your council or housing association home is a big decision and a commitment that shouldn't be taken lightly, or without seeking good advice.

In the accompanying leaflet you'll find more information on Right to Buy.

We'll tell you about the steps you'll need to take on your way towards home ownership, and some of the things you'll need to consider before making your decision.

Further information, support and advice, useful contacts and the Right to Buy application form are available on our website **communities.gov.uk/righttobuy**

If you'd like any questions answered before taking the next steps we'll be happy to help you. Simply call us on **0300 123 0913**.

Yours sincerely,

The Right to Buy Team

Like to buy your home?
Give us a call or visit our website to take the next steps towards owning your home.

I don't live in sheltered housing or other housing suitable for elderly or disabled people

...you could be eligible for up to **£75,000 discount**

0300 123 0913
communities.gov.uk/righttobuy